T0300255

Protective Operations

A Handbook for Security and Law Enforcement

Protective Operations

A Handbook for Security and Law Enforcement

Glenn P. McGovern

CRC Press
Taylor & Francis Group
Boca Raton   London   New York

CRC Press is an imprint of the
Taylor & Francis Group, an **informa** business

CRC Press
Taylor & Francis Group
6000 Broken Sound Parkway NW, Suite 300
Boca Raton, FL 33487-2742

International Standard Book Number: 978-1-4398-5171-5 (Hardback)

Library of Congress Cataloging-in-Publication Data
McGovern, Glenn.
Protective operations : a handbook for security and law enforcement / Glenn P. McGovern.
p. cm.
Includes bibliographical references and index.
ISBN 978-1-4398-5171-5 (alk. paper)
1. Protective custody. 2. Assassination--Prevention. 3. Kidnapping--Prevention. 4. Crime--Prevention. 5. Police patrol. I. Title.
HV8031.M35 2011
363.2'3--dc22   2010048797

Visit the Taylor & Francis Web site at
http://www.taylorandfrancis.com

and the CRC Press Web site at
http://www.crcpress.com

CONTENTS

PREFACE

Approximately nine years ago, after taking a position as a criminal investigator with the one of the largest district attorney offices in California, I became involved with the special operations group that was tasked primarily with conducting protective operations for the staff as well as victims, witnesses, and informants. As a former SWAT operator with my last department, it was a natural fit. At around the same time, another investigator was hired who had been a SWAT/sniper with his last department. Surprisingly for both us, of the approximate 10 investigators in the unit, only two others were former SWAT, one of whom was the soon to be commander of the unit. The rest of the team, while all very experienced law enforcement professionals, had limited specialized tactical training, the exceptions being a former army ranger and a former state narcotics special agent. Out of the whole team, only three of us, including myself, had attended a basic dignitary protection course.

Fortunately, the team had a wide selection of weaponry including fully automatic submachine guns in three different calibers, assault rifles, and shotguns with which to work. The training initially began with the basics, motorcade operations, and the various pedestrian protective rings. With access of a facility that allowed vehicles to be brought up on the firing range, as well as a large tire house, we were able to evolve the training to live fire scenarios. The problem that quickly became apparent was that there was not much information available on what to train for beyond the basics. Specifically, what type of attacks could be encountered by an individual and/or protective detail?

In 2002, in an effort to train the team to respond to real world threats, not just some hypothetical attack, I began researching targeted attacks from around the world, beginning with January 1950. In April of 2010, I published the first result of this research, *Targeted Violence: A Statistical and Tactical Analysis of Assassinations, Contract Killings, and Kidnappings* (CRC Press, 2010). This was a compilation and analysis of 900 targeted attacks on individuals, many of whom had protective teams. The attack information was broken down to individual elements to allow for ease of understanding. Since then, I have continued to monitor attacks occurring around the world. While many attacks have fallen into the statistical "norm" that I discovered during my early research, there also have been a fair amount of new and innovative tactics employed by government agents, criminals, and terrorists around the world. Out of this research, I, along with my team commander, Lt. Maurice Lane, developed tactics that allowed the team to respond to the more commonly employed methods of attack.

While admittedly many attack methods were rarely witnessed in the United States, there was a method to the madness. The United States is a great country and one of its greatest strengths is its very diverse population encompassing nearly every religion, race, and ethnicity to be found on Earth. While most bring what is best about their individual cultures and beliefs, unfortunately, the seedy underside also is present to some degree. Therefore, a protective team can never have a positive idea of what nature a threat might take. As such, I believed in training my team to effectively respond to the worst possible scenarios. This was only reinforced as I discovered that California was or had been home to KGB-trained assassins, South American death squad commandos, and the man who planned the bombings of the two United States embassies in East Africa.[1]

For some individuals, teams, command staff, and departments, this may present a problem, as there is an elevated degree of danger and liability that comes with training protective teams to a high level of efficiency. It is for each organization to make the decision as to what level of protection they wish to provide. I would only caution that law enforcement is not usually brought into the fold to provide protection in order to enhance an individual's perceived notoriety or importance. Law enforcement provides protection because it is believed, hopefully following a competent risk and threat assessment, that an individual is being targeted for murder. If the threat is any less, I am not sure law enforcement should be involved.

The nature of a targeted attack against a protected individual is in short, an ambush. Should it ever occur, the protective team will be in the fight of its life. The only chance of survival, beyond sheer dumb luck, will be if it has trained to respond immediately with extreme violence of action. If the team/agency is not prepared to do that, then perhaps it would be better if it was left to others to provide protection. If it were your loved one that was being targeted, what level of readiness and protection would you want a team to provide?

This work is the result of all of my training, research, and experience in protective operations at the law enforcement level, as well as the insights of many other professional lawmen. You will find that while there are many commonalities with protective work afforded to government dignitaries and corporate executives, there are also many differences. The goal was not to have all that I have learned be lost, but to provide it to others that will be tasked with the work in the future, but without revealing specific tactics. I hope you find it informative and are able to incorporate some of it into your own operations. Finally, I hope this is only a starting point and that you take from this and improve upon it.

ENDNOTE

1. Nikolai Khokhlov was a KGB-trained assassin who became famous by not carrying out the hit, but rather by approaching his target and explaining what he had been tasked to do. Eventually Khokhlov, after being relocated in the United States, became a professor at California State University in San Bernardino. In the early 2000s, a former El Salvadorian army officer was civilly sued for his involvement in the March 24, 1980, assassination of Archbishop Oscar Arnulfo Romero in El Salvador. During the 1990s, Ali Mohamed, a former officer in the Egyptian army and a man who trained Osama bin Laden's personal bodyguards and planned the bombings of the U.S. embassies in East Africa, was residing in a house in Santa Clara, California.

ACKNOWLEDGMENTS

Many years ago, early in my career I had the good fortune to attend training provided by members of the U.S. Army Special Forces. Its focus was on the methods used to eliminate sentries—techniques using knife, garrote, and suppressed weapons among other things. However, it was during a night training patrol that a single Special Forces soldier taught me a lesson I have never forgotten. While moving through a wooded area in a column formation, I suddenly felt a hand followed by a knife to my throat. The man's face, obscured by camouflage paint preventing any identification or recognition, faintly whispered, "You're dead," into my ear, before quickly and quietly moving farther up the line. Had this not been a training exercise, I would not be here today because I had along with many in my patrol violated a cardinal rule, we had failed to check our "six" (or, in laymen terms, failed to check what was coming up behind us).

In the more than 20 years since that night, I have continued to learn, to search out more training in order to deal with hostile actions. I have had the chance to train with and be trained by Army Special Forces, Navy SEALS, Australian SAS, Israeli commandos, CIA Case Officers, FBI SWAT and HRT, as well as law enforcement veterans from the NYPD, LAPD, and a host of others. The lessons have been many and remembered. This book could not have happened without the training, guidance, and influence I received from these individuals. To these men, and especially that unknown Special Forces soldier, I thank you for your dedication.

I also want to thank my mentor, Santa Clara County District Attorney Lieutenant Maurice Lane (Ret.), for his friendship and insight in reviewing this work, for the days of training in bitter cold and sweltering heat, and operations in the middle of the night in dangerous neighborhoods. A heartfelt thank you to Napa County District Attorney Chief Investigator Andy Mazzanti, San Diego County District Attorney Commander Wayne Maxey (Ret), Pacific Grove Police Detective Al Fasulo (Ret.), and Security and Intelligence Specialist Craig Schneider for their willingness to review this work and provide me with their comments, insights, and opinions, all of which I value greatly. Thank you all for your time and friendship.

To my editor, Mark Listewnik, thank you for your willingness to take a chance on a new author and for your continued support with a second book.

Of course, I would not be who I am today without the unending support of my family. To my parents, thank you for your love and guidance generously provided over the decades and, perhaps most importantly, the freedom to pursue my dreams and my own way in this life. To my beautiful bride, Christina, I would not be the man I am today without your friendship, love, and support. You are truly the perfect cop's wife. To my children who have been my greatest adventure in life, I love you dearly.

THE AUTHOR

Glenn McGovern is currently a senior investigator for one of the largest district attorney's offices in California. Over his 20-plus year career he has worked as a Special Deputy U.S. Marshal, police officer, deputy sheriff, and law enforcement specialist. It was as an 18-year-old member of the U.S. Air Force Security Police, just beginning his law enforcement career, that he was first introduced to the study of terrorism, tactical operations, and protective details. Europe at the time was on fire, as groups, such as the Sicilian mafia, November 17, Red Army Faction, Hezbollah, and many others, were conducting their terrorist attacks, many of which targeted U.S. military installations. As a newly minted law enforcement member assigned to a police unit that had a combat mission and was deployable worldwide, the study of the tactics used by these groups was mandatory.

It was also during his time in the U.S. Air Force that he had his first experiences with close personal protection operations, first with Soviet diplomats visiting under the Intermediate-Range Nuclear Forces (INF) Treaty, then later in Panama with the commanding general of all U.S. forces in South America. He was later involved in an unusual protective operation in which he was locked in with the protectee, which, in this case was over $16 million in cash en route to U.S. military installations in the Pacific.

Upon completion of his military service, he went to work for the Orange County Marshal's Department assigned to court house security as well as bailiff functions. Upon completing the Orange County Sheriff's Academy, he was assigned as a deputy sheriff working in the jails. Approximately two years later, he obtained a position with the Pacific Grove Police Department in Monterey County. While there, he worked as a patrolman, detective, and corporal.

He also held a collateral assignment as a member of the SWAT team for approximately six years. Although the Pacific Grove Police Department was small, as were many of the departments on the coast, being one of only three SWAT teams in the entire county, he had the opportunity to participate in a variety of operations, from hostage situations to barricaded gunmen as well as high-risk search/arrest warrant services. This assignment also led to his next major experience in providing protection, this time to President

xv

Bill Clinton and Vice President Al Gore, along with both first ladies during their visit to the Stanford University Ocean Research facility.

He later took a job with the bureau of investigation for a district attorney office in California, where he remains to this day. Here, he quickly became a member of the Special Operations Group tasked with protective operations for district attorney staff, primarily prosecutors, as well as victims and witnesses. It was as a member of this group that he became more involved in the nuances of protective work as well as the training of a protective team. In particular, he found that providing protection to victims and witnesses involved an issue with which most protective teams do not generally have to deal.

At times, the victim or witness being protected was a current or former member of an organized prison gang. As such, even when on the "outs" (meaning the individual was no longer in the good graces of the gang), that person was in a position to see the methods of operation, equipment, members of teams, and how they operate. As anyone who has worked organized crime, and gangs in particular, can attest, it does not take much for a gang member to get back in the good graces of his gang, and as a result, bring with him the inside knowledge of the protective operations of the DA's office.

While with the District Attorney's Office, McGovern was assigned full-time to the FBI's Joint Terrorism Task Force as a Special Deputy United States Marshal, conducting international terrorism investigations for a period of three years. In this assignment, he conducted counterterrorism investigations into a variety of groups, including some that have carried out targeted killings. He also was able to attend training that included the construction and detonation of a 500-lb ammonium nitrate and fuel oil (ANFO) vehicle car bomb, as well as dealing with suicide bombers, which provided him unique insight into how these operations could be carried out.

He holds a bachelor's degree in criminal justice from the Union Institute in Ohio as well as a certificate in crime and intelligence analysis from California State University, Sacramento. He is the author of *Targeted Violence: A Statistical and Tactical Analysis of Assassinations, Contract Killings, and Kidnappings* (CRC Press, 2010). He also has authored several articles dealing with intelligence, targeted attack analysis, and SWAT-related subjects in periodicals, such as *Law and Order, The Counter Terrorist, Police,* and the *Journal of Counterterrorism & Homeland Security International.* He also speaks on the issue of protective operations, specifically situational awareness, operational security, surveillance detection, and the tactics employed in these types of attacks.

INTRODUCTION

If anything, overestimate the opposition. Certainly never underestimate it. But do not let that lead to nervousness or lack of confidence. Don't get rattled, and know that with hard work, calmness, and by never irrevocably compromising yourself, you can always, always best them.

Allen Dulles
Director, CIA (1953–1961)

In researching over 1000 targeted attacks that have occurred over the past 60 years, I found that in only 305 of the attacks was a protective detail of some configuration present.[1] In the vast majority of those, the protective detail was constituted by police officers. During that same time period, 87 police officers have been specifically targeted by hostile organizations. All told, of the 1000-plus attacks, the adversary was successful over 81 percent of the time (the victim was killed and/or kidnapped).

Throughout the history of law enforcement, police officers have often been called upon to provide protective services for individuals believed to be in danger of physical harm. Most often this service has been provided to the victims and witnesses involved in criminal cases, but more and more often it includes mayors, local elected officials, prosecutors, and judges. For a large number of protective operations, this level of training and experience has and will continue to suffice, as many of those that seek to kill or harm another will not attempt to take on a police officer, let alone several. However, in those cases where the adversary is dedicated, the presence of police officers may not be enough, as has been witnessed most recently in Mexico. In these types of attack scenarios, the level of training of the average officer will be far from sufficient.

Unlike protective operations normally conducted by the U.S. Secret Service and the Department of State or even corporate security organizations, law enforcement agencies at the county and municipal level are often tasked to provide protection to a wide variety of individuals. These individuals can range from witnesses, informants, and victims, to their own office leaders and staff, even local government representatives. Regardless of the protectee or the nature of the threat, law enforcement officers, as is the norm for the profession, are expected to rise to the occasion and handle the problem.

Interesting enough, this tendency to reach out to law enforcement for assistance in providing protection continues when the officers retire and delve into private detective work. A good example of this occurred recently when a colleague of mine called one evening for some advice on running a protective operation. Now, this is a man who was a highly dedicated police officer until he was forced to retire for medical reasons and is now a dedicated private detective. However, he was not prior military, never a part of any SWAT team or similar tactical unit, nor had he even attended a basic protection course. He was tapped for the assignment because he was a known entity to the area, could be counted on, and was authorized to be armed with a concealed weapon.

My colleague informed me that he would be running the detail by himself with only the assistance of a locally hired limousine chauffeur and that it was set to go the following day. The answer to my first question of who the protectee was stunned me when he advised that it was a senior member of former President George W. Bush's team. This man had made a considerable number of enemies and seemed to be despised almost globally. My friend and I started to discuss the operation and his preparation. He was initially going to be equipped as though he was going back on patrol. He had not conducted any threat assessment, site survey, or route analysis, which was more due to a lack of mission-specific knowledge rather than time. Fortunately, the operation went without incident, but after a 15-hour day, my friend had learned a lot, all by way of "on the job" training. Unfortunately, this is not an isolated occurrence.

In a perfect world, every protective team would have three or more armored vehicles of the same make and model. All would be secured in a location that prevents hostile tampering. All drivers would be trained and experienced in evasive driving and counter ambush skills. A group of skilled analysts and operators would carry out a complete and competent protective advance and site surveys as well as threat and risk assessment prior to every operation. While this is characteristic of the large state and federal agencies, unfortunately, for many law enforcement agencies—even the larger, better-funded ones—this is not the norm. The reality is that law enforcement agencies are often asked to provide protection with little to no job-oriented training and with few resources to accomplish the mission in the most effective and safest method. The key, then, is to work with the available vehicle resources and funding to reach the goals and provide a professional level of service that the public expects.

When the term "protective operations" is used, it is conceivable that most of society would conjure images of large, suited bodyguards with dark sunglasses and motorcades. While certainly a factor of protective work, in reality it encompasses much, much more. What passes for protection at the corporate level will differ from that at the law enforcement level, which differs still from that of a federal agency, such as the Secret Service. Further, there are different levels or classifications of protection. For instance, perhaps the lowest level of the protection spectrum would be providing information necessary for an individual to be more knowledgeable of situational awareness. The next could be a professional threat assessment by a government agency or corporation to determine if a threat exists.

From there, protection, depending upon threat, could include special parking, home security surveys, concealed weapons, and perhaps temporary installation of closed-circuit television (CCTV). Next on the protection ladder would be a protective detail of some sort. This could run the gamut between only during work hours to 24 hours a day, 7 days a week. It could be one agent or a full team—and anywhere in between. Beyond this, the protective operation moves into the realm of safe houses and even new identities.

The point is that protective operations, if they are going to be provided in a professional and effective manner, require the incorporation of a variety of skill sets. While there are many books on the market that deal with providing executive protection and/or threat assessment, this work seeks to fill identified gaps. Its goal is to be a reference for law enforcement and security organizations tasked with a protective role, but with limited resources and training, as seems to often be the case. This work also has the goal of providing a basic outline on dealing with the worst-case scenario and, more importantly, training to deal with it should it ever occur.

This work will to identify those issues particular to local law enforcement and, to a degree, private security teams that may be called in later, and offer suggestions and guidance. The goal is not to delve into specific tactics, such as motorcade operations, protective rings, etc., as much of this has been covered in detail in other published works (some of which are suggested in Chapter 4 and Appendix A). Further, tactics are better learned firsthand and, in the author's opinion, should not be covered in open-source material. A large portion of what is presented stems from my training and experiences as well as discussions with colleagues in providing protection to a diverse set of protectees and circumstances, all with limited manpower and resources.

ENDNOTE

1. This stems from research conducted for my first book, *Targeted Violence: A Statistical and Tactical Analysis of Assassinations, Contract Killings, and Kidnappings,* in addition to my ongoing monitoring of such attacks occurring around the world.

1

Breaking the Mindset

> If you're not shootin', you should be loadin'. If you're not loadin', you should be movin', if you're not movin', someone's gonna cut your head off and put it on a stick.
>
> **Clint Smith**
> *Director of Thunder Ranch*

Law enforcement officers, be they a cop on patrol, a detective or a federal agent working a case, all are "wired" by either their nature or their training to look for and deal with trouble. The same can be said of individuals in the higher end of the security profession. Combined, all of us represent the thin line of defense against society's malefactors. It is not in our DNA to run from a fight, and perhaps more to the point, no one else is prepared to deal with the problem. When the violence starts and people are fleeing in terror, it is the men and women wearing the badge that swallow their fear and charge into the situation. This is even truer of individuals in aggressive specialized units such as gang enforcement, narco units and of course, SWAT teams.

One of the greatest examples of this "calling" occurred during a shootout in North Hollywood, California. On February 28, 1997, two men wearing head-to-toe body armor used automatic weapons to engage police officers of the Los Angeles Police Department in a running gun battle that lasted forty-four minutes during which over 2,000 rounds were fired. It was a scene straight out of the news footage of Iraq, yet was in our own backyard. Unfortunately, in recent years it has been repeated in places such as Mumbai, India, and Ciudad Juarez, Mexico.

As with any profession, not everyone performs his or her job the same way or with the same degree of efficiency. As in anyone in law enforcement can attest, just because an individual wears a badge and a weapon does not mean they can protect another human being under attack. There are many sub functions in modern law enforcement and while all have the goal of protecting the public and capturing the bad guy, not all go about it in the same fashion. There are those that are drawn to the crime prevention aspects, or the school resource officer, SWAT, or even those that enjoy straight patrol for their career. The point is not every officer can do or rather should do every job in law enforcement.

Conducting protective operations is no different. While it shares the attributes of a SWAT team, an intelligence unit and even a crisis response team, it requires a different mindset than these traditional specialties incorporate individually. This is not to say that officers with this background and experience should not be involved in protective operations, quite the contrary. The point is that protective operations are unique in law enforcement. It is a function that police officers are often called upon to handle while being perhaps one of the least prepared for.

Law enforcement and security officers have months of training, a duty belt laden with the tools to accomplish the job, excellent communication (most times) allowing for backup to be called at a moment's notice. As such, they are well prepared for the job. With this background, it stands to reason then that cops can and should perform the function of providing protection to others who are being specifically targeted. Does it not fall within the very parameters of their profession? For the most part the answer is yes, however there are factors that need to be considered, in some cases modified and dealt with.

For law enforcement officers on a protective assignment, a certain degree of the "cop mindset" must be changed. In its place would be the development of the "combat mindset," which is what would be required when dealing with a worst-case ambush scenario. Hence the title of this chapter, there are certain aspects to protective operations that run counter to the ingrained training of the law enforcement and security professional. The foremost of these deals with the primary goal of any protective detail, that of keeping the principal safe from harm. This means that at the first signs of trouble, the cops in the protective detail need to avoid and move in the opposite direction. This "running away" can be extremely difficult for some officers to deal with. While they understand the reasoning, it runs counter to their professional and personal philosophy, and possibly most difficult, counter to their instinct.

In protective work, the mission is to move the principal from point A to point B without incident. However, should an ambush occur, the protective detail's function is to break contact with the attack and evacuate the protectee to a location of safety. Continuing the counterattack against the adversary is generally the wrong move, one that could result in you or your principal being killed or badly injured. In an ambush scenario, successfully breaking contact is the challenge. The military trains teams to "push through" or forward out of the kill zone. However, in some cases, retreating out of the area is the best response. The word retreat is not usually a concept that comes easily for members of law enforcement to learn or accept, yet it is sometimes what is required.

The concepts of combat differ significantly from what are normally found in the law enforcement community. Cops and security traditionally work in teams of two or solo. Moving as a team requires a separate set of skills, foreign to many without a military or SWAT background. Yet in protective operations, they are a key component. Perhaps one of the most basic of all military tactics is the concept of cover fire, or shooting in the direction of an adversary so team members can move to cover. This may include engaging an adversary in a sustained manner while moving in the opposite direction. In the case of an ambush, it can be absolutely critical to a team's survivability. Yet cover fire runs counter to traditional law enforcement training, practice and doctrine that requires engaging a specific threat.

Another aspect of breaking the mindset is with the issue of surveillance detection. We cops are so used to being the hunters that we can easily forget that we can become victims too. While there are plenty of schools for cops on the proper ways to conduct surveillance, there are very few that teach its detection. Like anything worth learning, it takes time and practice. Ironically, with the proper motivation and willpower, it is something that can and should be incorporated into a cop's daily routine. Ideally, they should get in the habit of surveying their surroundings anytime they step into the public arena. While one would think this is already ingrained, it is surprising how oblivious cops can be.

Some of this can be attributed to the current assignment of the officer. For cops and security on patrol it would be nearly impossible to carry out ongoing mobile surveillance detection, given the varied nature of patrol travel patterns, there could be little reason for an adversary to carry out such surveillance. Hence, there would be little reason or practicality to learn it. However, for those assigned to counter such activity as narcotics, gangs and terrorism or assigned to an intelligence unit should continuously practice the detection of surveillance. It is when operating a vehicle—the area least trained in and therefore requiring the most practice—that surveillance detection offers the greatest benefits. For these individuals, if assigned to a protective unit as perhaps a collateral assignment, the correct mindset would already be in place.

Another issue comes in the form of equipment. Most police officers are used to having a multitude of instruments on their waist, or in the car within close reach. SWAT teams deployed in a protective function generally operate with a full equipment turnout. For those conducting a more covert protective function, much of this gear is not needed and in most instances is not applicable to the job. This is because the "enforcement" function of police work is not necessary in the protective role.

The baton, the stun gun, pepper spray all constitute levels of force an officer may select from in order to enforce the law, overcome resistance and affect an arrest. On a protective detail with the different set of priorities, the equipment requirement changes. The reason for law enforcement involvement is that a threat on the life of an individual is believed to exist. This means that those individuals on a protective detail need to focus on the scenarios they are most likely to face, i.e., the ambush. The basic equipment requirements then entail a firearm and ammunition, a flashlight, a small knife and a small first aid kit geared towards dealing with gunshot trauma.

Those assigned to a protective function need to understand the difference in tactics and equipment. More importantly, train to acquire the skills and confidence to deal with an ambush. This is not about courage or cowardice, but rather accomplishing the mission at hand. In the coming chapters, we will discuss all of this and more. In the end, it is up to you the reader as either an operational member or a manager to make the final determination as to what type of team, if any, will be fielded.

2

Policy and Procedure Considerations

Bravery is being the only one who knows you're afraid.

Col. David H. Hackworth

While the exact title may differ, just about every professional law enforcement agency in the civilized world has some form of operational guidelines. In the United States, it is a necessity-given the litigious society in which cops find themselves. However, the depth of coverage these policy and procedure manuals provide varies widely. This is especially true when dealing with protective operations, which, while having a history in police work, are not generally considered when the manuals are written. In the following pages are described specific ways in which protective details responding to emergency situations, such as an ambush, can find themselves in violation of the procedures or codes of conduct. The goal of this chapter is to make teams and administrations aware of potential problems and provide language that may serve as possible solutions. Prior to implementing any policy changes, always consult with a city or county attorney.

USE OF FORCE

The first policy that has the most to do with a team's response to any ambush is a department's Use of Force policy. It is generally within this section that they would expect to find the rules and regulations to which they are held accountable during the performance of their job. A common subsection deals with the issue of shooting at or from a moving vehicle. Many police departments address in some form or fashion shooting at a fleeing vehicle. Generally, it is discouraged unless the vehicle is being used as a weapon and shooting at it is for protection of self or others and only when there is no other means of eliminating the threat. The issue some departments bring up when shooting at a vehicle is the potential of the driver becoming disabled. While this would be the obvious objective of shooting at a vehicle in order to eliminate the threat, should the driver in fact be disabled, the vehicle could become an uncontrollable deadly weapon.

This issue could certainly come up, however, in protective operations; it is exceedingly unlikely that an adversary attacking a protective operation would act alone while at the same time driving a vehicle. However, should this be the case, and depending on the region the operation is occurring in and the adversary, the concern may be that the driver is, in fact, a suicide bomber in a vehicle-borne improvised explosive device (VBIED). Police officers are always authorized to use deadly force to protect themselves or others, but with such policies in place, theoretically, should they be engaged in a drive-by fashion (a far more likely attack scenario), they would be violating the shooting at a moving vehicle prohibition if they responded in kind.

One of the reasons for the prohibition is the difficulty of successfully engaging a moving vehicle. Ideally, one should take cover. However, if caught in the open, there may be little choice. This policy is understandable from the point of view of most uniformed officers. However, for protective teams dealing with a carload of adversaries actively attacking with firearms, it falls far short. While there is no argument regarding the difficulty of hitting a moving target accurately, it can be done. For protective teams, just as with other special operations units, training for this should be a standard. As such, the policy should accommodate this.

A less common section of a policy and procedure manual on "use of force" is shooting from a moving vehicle. Given the difficulty of accurate shot placement coupled with the normal lack of training in such tactics, it is largely prohibited, if covered at all. While it is easy to understand the reasoning behind the prohibition, for protective details it could present some liability problems, at least for the officer. Statistically, the majority of ambushes on motorcades take the form of shooting attacks.[1] In response to such attacks, protective members could easily find themselves having to return fire while their vehicle driver is attempting to escape the area. Rather than prohibiting it altogether, a better option to consider is to allow shooting from a moving vehicle if properly trained and only in self-defense or defense of others and when there is no other perceivable means of avoidance.

The Pinellas County Sheriff's Department in Arizona is one of the few agencies known to have dealt with the issue by detailing it within the general orders on use of force. The title of the section is "Use of Force in Motor Vehicle Situations" and states, "Shooting at or from a moving vehicle shall be avoided in all circumstances except those which do not endanger innocent persons and are justified by unusual or exigent circumstances." The section continues with a note that states, "Emphasize that when shooting at a motor vehicle … being used as a deadly weapon, that the target is not the vehicle itself, but the driver who is using the vehicle as an instrumentality of deadly force. Therefore, deputies should not be firing at the engine block or tire to stop a threat."

While the foregoing covers the issue of shooting from or at a vehicle in an ambush situation, it does not allow an officer to shoot at the vehicle. If a team is armed with a large enough caliber and is trained in disabling a vehicle, then this prevents it from effectively stopping the threat. However, it would only take a slight modification for a department to allow such responses in general, with certain exceptions.

One of the more rare policies found (and in the author's opinion, very progressive) that directly relates to a protective function is one detailing the concept of "cover fire."[2] The policy states that the wording "other authorized uses for firearms" includes cover fire, which it defines as "the discharge of a firearm in a tactical situation to neutralize the use of deadly force (by the adversary). Cover fire is not intended to strike a subject, but is meant only to prevent subjects from taking action against police officers."

This is an extremely interesting policy, as it would appear to fly in the face of what most officers are held accountable for by their departments; that is, no warning shots and to be aware of your backstop (i.e., who is behind the adversary that could be injured) when engaging a specific threat. At the same time, however, cover fire can be a critical component for a team attempting to disengage itself from an ambush. The department with this policy clearly recognized this need, although it is not specifically related to protective work and, so, detailed the rules on its use, thereby providing their officers the flexibility in methods of response, while still setting guidelines.

LEAVING THE SCENE OF A SHOOTING

This topic is rarely addressed by law enforcement agencies, as, perhaps due to the nature of the job, the thought of leaving the scene of a shooting by a police officer is inconceivable. Short of being involved in a shooting of a fleeing felon, most law enforcement-encountered shootings occur during traffic stops or fixed locations, such as a residence or place of business. Law enforcement personnel do not by their nature retreat from a threat; instead, they call in reinforcements. Even in the aforementioned North Hollywood shootout, while the movement and firing resulting in a very large crime scene, the officers involved never left the scene. When a protective detail is ambushed, the resulting chaos could be considerable. Consider the following scenario (one that has been repeated throughout the history of targeted attacks).

A protective detail operating in a covert fashion is moving through the city. At a secondary traffic intersection controlled by a stop sign, the detail is ambushed by two vehicles with four to six shooters. One of the hostile vehicles is crashed into the protective detail during an intercept move. The protective detail immediately return fire successfully, injuring or killing several of the attackers as the security driver is able to make an escape out of the area. Responding police officers find the crashed vehicle as well as bodies (including possible injured innocent civilians) lying around. With no clue as to what occurred, except perhaps a vague witness-provided description of events, an alert is put out on the radio. The protective detail made up of police officers has the mission to get the principal to a place of safety. Obviously, they would later return to the scene of the attack, but that could take some time and describing the events could no doubt be a challenge.

The general lack of communication could be decreased if the police protective detail was within its own jurisdiction or within an area with common radio coverage. However, when a team is operating outside its jurisdiction, it is entirely conceivable for a great amount of confusion to result. While an exceedingly rare scenario, it is not without precedent and, therefore, should be addressed in some fashion. (A word of caution: In dealing with this potential issue, a team's operational security should not be compromised—see more in Chapter 7.)

DUTY TO PROVIDE MEDICAL ATTENTION

Another common part of use of force policies details providing medical attention following the application of force. In the case of a protective team being attacked, this is simply not feasible. A caveat to this section could state something to that effect. Another option was selected by a police department that stated that, "in those cases where the person injured can be provided medical attention and there is no risk to the life of an officer, and when such action is tactically feasible, such medical attention should be provided." Again, flexibility is provided with a set of guidelines.

LEAVING THE SCENE OF A COLLISION

Similar to leaving the scene of a shooting is leaving the scene of a traffic collision. Whether due to hostile attack or legitimate accidental traffic collision, a protective detail cannot remain on scene. Rather, it must secure the principal prior to returning to the location. If the accident is legitimate and there are multiple vehicles within a motorcade, one car could conceivably remain on scene until the protectee is secured. Otherwise, the motorcade should proceed and return to the scene once the protectee is secured. Regardless, as with other portions of this chapter, flexibility within guidelines is the ideal.

USE OF IMPACT WEAPONS AND PEPPER SPRAY

In the author's opinion, these weapons have limited use in protective operations because the critical need when encountering an adversary is to break contact and move the protectee to an area of safety. However, some departments or teams may choose to implement them. Further, in many policy and procedure manuals, once pepper spray has been deployed, the officer is required to stay on scene and even render first aid, once the suspect is secured. This is not what a protective member needs to be doing. Should a team decide to have the team members use such weapons, their medical aid should be commensurate with that detailed under shooting incidents.

Along these same lines is the issue of less lethal weapons, such as Tasers™ and beanbag-type weapons. As with the pepper spray and impact weapons, the goal is to obtain compliance in order to affect an arrest. These weapons are designed for that very reason, and their use in a protective detail would be extremely rare, if ever. Certainly, there is always a potential scenario, but as the studies on targeted attacks against a protective detail indicate, their use is nullified by the use of firearms and explosives by the hostile adversary.

EMERGENCY VEHICLE USE

Emergency vehicle use and, in particular, vehicle pursuits, are another major section in most policy and procedure manuals. However, few, if any, cover instances in which it is the officer who is being pursued. While not specifically mentioned, one department did include a category titled "Restricted Pursuits," which it defined as those that fall out of the category of the "traditional" pursuit, and how they should be handled. This is perhaps the ideal area for a policy and procedure manual to cover the subject of a protective detail being pursued by a hostile adversary.

Terrorists and criminals who would carry out a targeted attack know that the longer the duration of the engagement, the more likely it is that reinforcements will arrive, resulting in their identification and capture. As such, any pursuit of a protective detail motorcade is most likely to be very limited. In terms of a protective detail evading a hostile pursuer, a pursuit has indeed begun, only the roles of the players have switched. As such, the language detailing the evasion of a hostile party could be similar to the pursuit policy, but in reverse. Something as simple as "when officers on a protective detail are attempting to evade a threat, emergency lights and siren will be employed (which also assists in bringing attention to the attack). When determined that the immediate threat has abated, officers will continue to the nearest safe location while continuing to observe other drivers," etc.

CODE 3 EQUIPMENT

A part of the section on vehicle use should be a section describing the use of Code 3 equipment on motorcade details. All law enforcement vehicles used in such a fashion need to be fully Code 3 equipped: lights and siren. In the event of an attack, the use of the Code 3 equipment will attract a lot of attention, including perhaps nearby police in marked units. Further, and more important, it covers the officers (in terms of liability) while they maneuver their vehicles at increased speeds.

Another often-seen section under vehicle use is that dealing with seat belts. Generally, most departments require their officers to use seat belts during the normal use of police vehicles. Some may argue that in a protective motorcade there is the issue of hindering quick access to one's weapon. While that is certainly a possibility, motorcade operations are run with a minimum of two operators, and if they are alert, then they should be able to unbuckle the seat belt at the first indications of a threat. Also, if the driver conducts high-speed evasive maneuvers in an attempt to flee, not having a seat belt on could be dangerous. Ultimately, each team needs to have a discussion and make a decision, and each department should allow the officers the flexibility.

QUALIFIED IMMUNITY

The use of Code 3 equipment in pursuits and in fleeing hostile attacking forces brings up the question of immunity for the law enforcement officer. In California, and most likely in many if not all other states, law enforcement vehicles responding to an emergency or chasing a fleeing suspect are required to employ lights and siren. This, coupled with taking reasonable precautions for the public's safety when in this situation, is what is needed to protect the amount of liability a law enforcement officer could face if he or she were involved in a traffic collision. Due to some recent dramatic collisions involving officers, this issue has been a hot topic of discussion for the general public as well as state senators. The question then becomes, does this protection extend to law enforcement officers driving at high speed to evade an attacking force even if they are operating with the lights and siren?

SPECIALIZED VEHICLE USES

Under the pursuit or vehicle operations section, often the issues of ramming and the Pursuit Immobilization Technique, or "PIT maneuver," as well as evasive escape maneuvers are commonly covered. One department's policy had the following language:

> Officers will **not** consider employing any type of intervention tactic such as blocking, ramming, or boxing the fleeing vehicle. Officers will **not** use additional methods of intervention that may include PIT (Pursuit Immobilization Technique); such maneuvers create an extreme risk to all persons involved in the pursuit and to all persons in the immediate area.

The problem with the foregoing policy and procedure is that, in the event of a hostile attack on a protective detail, many, if not all, of these techniques would have to be used for the detail to escape physical injury. The policy is strict, giving the officer no flexibility, and it thereby potentially prevents an officer in a protective detail from employing a method of evasion due to in direct violation of the policy and procedure manual. This could result in punishment at the department level, or worse, civil legal action should an injury occur.

While many of the evasive maneuvers taught to protective or special operations teams, such as the reverse or forward 180s and the J-turn, are not generally covered in a typical policy and procedure manual, there is not usually an issue regarding employing them. However, most departments employ cover pursuits and the PIT technique. As a result of injuries and fatalities sustained by innocent parties due to police pursuits, many departments have significantly restricted and, in some cases, outright forbidden its use. The same holds true for use of the PIT maneuver, let alone a reverse PIT technique.

One department, however, has provided the officers with the needed flexibility. The manual details the use of the PIT maneuver requiring a supervisor's approval, but adding the key component of "when time permits." It also states only those trained in the PIT maneuver may employ it.

The aspect of using an emergency vehicle to ram another vehicle is detailed by some departments. One department indicated that at speeds above 45 mph, it is considered deadly force and thus falls under the use of force guidelines. Whether this means if used against a person or another vehicle is unclear, but ultimately each department needs to come to its own determination (refer to Chapter 3 on issues of ramming a vehicle).

SPECIALIZED WEAPON USE

It is understood that protective teams should have access to specialized weapons, such as submachine guns and assault rifles. While they are becoming more commonly known as, "patrol rifles," their use is still highly controlled. Some police departments have created policies specifically dealing with special weapons. It is in the nature of protective operations that team members could find themselves facing the threat of an exceedingly well-armed adversary intent on killing the protectee and all who stand in their way. To forbid the use of specialized weapons, such as a rifle or submachine gun, puts that team at risk and questions the rationalé of that department's fielding a protective team in the first place. While in most instances team members will be able to carry out their protective assignment armed only with a sidearm, there are going to be times, hopefully as a result of a threat/risk assessment, when members should carry heavier firepower.

How a department handles the use of specialized weapons is obviously up to the chief. In the author's opinion, obtaining the chief's approval for deployment of such weapons is not a problem. However, to allow flexibility, there should be some language in the policy that allows the team commander to make the decision on issues in the absence of the chief, assistant chief, or similar department head. As part of this section, it should detail the minimum amount of initial training required for use, followed by what is determined to be necessary to maintain a qualification.

During my time as the team leader of my department's protective function, we started each training with a qualification in the use of submachine guns and assault rifles. This idea was stolen from an FBI SWAT team, but it was logical and allowed for each team member to always be "qualified" even if they should miss a training date. This is a Keep It Simple Stupid (KISS) way of dealing with a potentially hot button issue.

EXPLOSIVE DEVICE INCIDENTS

Explosive-based attacks are another issue that is commonly dealt with by protective details. Improvised explosive devices (IEDs) sent through the mail, positioned on the side of the road, in a car, or strapped to a person's body, all have been deployed against a protected person. While thankfully in the United States, Canada, and Mexico, the use of such methods has been a relatively rare occurrence, they are not without precedence,[3] including the use of a suicide bomber. For law enforcement agencies, the predominant experience with explosives has been the isolated pipe bomb or bomb-making equipment discovered during search warrants or placed at abortion clinics. The goal then has been to contain the area and immediately begin a search for potential secondary devices.

For protective operations, in the case of explosive attacks, the goal of the surviving parties is to evacuate the area to get the protectee to a secure area. This could very well mean leaving injured team members and civilians behind (see more in Chapter 4 on members providing their own trauma care). The use of explosives to initiate an ambush is a common method of operation, one taught and trained in by military units around the world (remember you may never completely know your adversary's background). Hence, tactically speaking, the team should not stop to deal with fires, triage centers, cordons, etc., but rather must escape the area and call for assistance.

In the urban setting, first responder response will be relatively quick, thus negating the need to provide medical attention to injured civilians; however, there will always be those that second-guess the decision, especially the team members themselves having to leave fallen comrades behind. If the decision to evacuate the scene and leave the injured in such instances is made for a team in the policy and procedure manual, perhaps it could lessen to some degree the "Monday morning quarterbacking," and perhaps team guilt, should a fellow operator fall.

One final aspect of dealing with explosive incidents is that of a suicide bomber. Relatively few law enforcement agencies have tackled the issue of how to respond and handle such a case. The suicide bomber is a lethal weapon in and of itself. Whether by means of triggering the device on command, by way of a dead man's switch, or some individual a safe distance away able to trigger the device remotely, a police or security officer will never know with any certainty the absolutely correct step to take. As a deadly force threat, a law enforcement officer would be justified in using deadly force. However, depending on the sensitivity of the explosive—many terrorists use an improvised formula—the shock of a bullet could cause the device to detonate. One approach discussed has been shooting at the head in order to kill the suspect prior to detonation.

This certainly could work, provided the shot placement was correct. The problem lies in that in most suicide bomber attacks, the device has been concealed under clothing. For protective details, this presents a major obstacle. Suicide bombers have been documented many times using a ruse to close the distance prior to detonation of the device. Should a protective team believe that an individual approaching its motorcade or protective ring is, in fact, a suicide bomber, how does it react? Unfortunately, there is no one correct answer, as was seen in the killing of a suspected suicide bomber by an armed member of the Metropolitan Police in London (immediately following the terrorist bombing of their Underground system), where it was discovered later that the suspect was not armed. All teams should spend some time discussing this type of attack and how they should respond.

ENDNOTES

1. In the over 1000 targeted attacks the author studied between January 1950 and September 2010, 345 were perpetrated against targets in transit. Of those, the vast majority were shooting-based ambushes.
2. Portland Police Bureau Manual of Policy and Procedure, January 2010.
3. In the author's research, there have been a total of nine explosive-based targeted attacks in North America. The recent bombings in Mexico, however, provide a clear indication of an escalation of violence that could change the statistical picture in North America of such attack methods.

3

Weapons, Vehicles, and Equipment

If you find yourself in a fair fight, you didn't plan your mission properly.

Col. David H. Hackworth
U.S. Army (Retd.)

The use of police officers in a direct protective role is a logical use of a resource by a law enforcement agency. Departments have the authority to allocate resources, such as manpower, vehicles, and equipment, to accomplish the mission. However, in protective operations, just being a trained police officer will most likely not be sufficient if a detail is ever attacked. Protective units, just like narco/intelligence units and SWAT teams, need specialized equipment and training. This even applies to SWAT teams that are periodically tasked with a protective function, as the nature of the mission is drastically different from their traditional role.

The issue of weapons often can be a hot button topic for a department or security company when discussing the needs, uses, expense, etc., and coupled with real or imagined liability. It is the author's opinion that when law enforcement-provided protection is brought into the equation, it is because someone's life is believed to be in immediate danger, not because someone lost his or her temper or felt hurt. To counter a legitimate threat, officers should have at their disposal a variety of tools, that is, weapons, to accomplish their mission in the safest way. At a minimum, an officer assigned to a protective detail will be armed with a handgun, preferably a pistol with several magazines.

In the vast majority of operations, a handgun will suffice, augmented by a small flashlight fitted with a strike cap and perhaps pepper spray. There will, however, be those occasions, due to the nature of the known or perceived threat, when additional firepower will be called for. This generally means either submachine guns and assault-type rifles, although shotguns also have their uses.

Since the 1950s, there have been four targeted attacks in the United States that are "known" to have employed automatic weapons (assault rifles or submachine guns). Worldwide, that number increases to 133; however, it is most probably substantially higher. Further, in North America, mostly due to the extreme violence in Mexico as a result of the drug cartels, the use of automatic weapons is on the rise.[1] Even in the urban streets of the United States, it is not uncommon to recover a Tech 9 auto pistol, a weapon capable of accepting a 50-round magazine with a rate of fire approaching 1000 rounds per minute. Even more disturbing is the increasing trend of police officers seizing SKS- and AK-47-type weapons following arrests and during the execution of search warrants.

BASIC EQUIPMENT

While the clothes for the team will change depending on the type of protectee (i.e., criminal informant, judge, agency head), the basic equipment and how it is worn should be standardized. (However, given the type of operation and the officer's position in the detail, this may need to be modified.) Body armor, weapon, ammunition, a flashlight, and a small trauma kit should be the minimum basic equipment. A phrase the author has often heard spoken from former U.S. Marines goes something like this: "Two is one, and one is none." The reference is to the need for redundancy in equipment supplies to account for Murphy's law. To ensure this, take a look at with what a protective detail goes operational. Is there anything that is mission critical, but you have only one? If so, determine how to double up on that identified need.

PISTOL

Depending on the department's policy, this weapon either is issued or, in some departments, the individual can make a selection, albeit from a specific caliber and manufacture. Without getting into the debate on superior

Figure 3.1   The 1911 (in all its variants) (top) and the H&K USP (bottom) are two formidable weapons firing the .45 ACP round. They are of similar size and weight, and yet the H&K holds 12 rounds compared to the 1911's traditional 7-round magazine.

calibers, protection work requires a solid round, but perhaps more importantly, the multiple rounds feature. Hence, while the venerable .45 caliber may be the officer's preference, some consideration needs to be given to the type of weapon system to use. Primarily, is the weapon concealable? A Colt model 1911 has many aficionados (including the author), but it may not be the best weapon for a protective operation. A more modern system in .45 caliber, but capable of holding 12–15 rounds in a relatively compact package, is probably better (Figure 3.1).

SUBMACHINE GUNS

Submachine guns are an ideal tool, well situated for protective work. Their small size and high ammo capacity, coupled with their ability to fire full auto, are advantageous to a protective detail in several ways. With the advent of magazine connecters, it is possible to have one weapon with between 40 and 60 rounds. Additionally, the nature of the weapon enables the shooter to effectively engage targets at a greater range than a pistol, even out to 100 meters (for some of the larger models). Continuing development within the industry is allowing for teams to have access to more compact weapons with higher ammunition count availability. Further, some of these weapon calibers can even penetrate body armor, which would be useful against a sophisticated adversary. By concealing such a weapon system under a sports coat, a team can maintain a very low profile without compromising on firepower.

LONG GUNS

In the United States, the M4 rifle can, and should, be used in protective operations. It is a weapon system that is capable of high rates of fire, but, more importantly, can accurately reach threats at 400 meters. As with submachine guns, the use of magazine connectors coupled with a butt stock magazine holder permits as many as 91 rounds, all in a single contained unit.

A 7.62 mm rifle also could be very useful, especially now that the length of some of these weapons has been significantly reduced. The Springfield SOCOM II and the H&K 417 are short in length and yet pack the power to stop chasing vehicles with a well-placed radiator or driver hit. The added benefit of a short 5.56 or 7.62 mm rifle is its ability to penetrate body armor. While there are no statistics on the use of body armor among assassins (although it is being increasingly used by Mexican drug cartels), it stands to reason that the more professional the hit team or individual, the better the chance of its use (depending, of course, on the type of attack to be carried out). Obviously, the use of ceramic plates could defeat these rounds, but the blunt force trauma inflicted by such rounds could have a preventative effect.

Weapons for consideration—and this is by no means a complete list—include:

H&K 417, 7.62 caliber, 12 or 16 in. barrel, weight 9.62 or 10.16 lb, measuring 31.69–34.84 to 35.62–38.77 in. in length.

H&K 416, 5.56 mm, 10.39 in. barrel, weight 7.21 lb, measuring 27.60–31.38 in. in length.

H&K G36C, 5.56 mm, 8.97 in. barrel, weight 6.52 lb, measuring 19.69–28.36 in. in length.

H&K UMP or MP-5K with either no stock or collapsible stock.

Figure 3.2 The SOCOM II puts the power of the 7.62 in a very compact package capable of being deployed inside of a vehicle.

H&K MP7A1, 4.6 × 3 mm, 7.08 in. barrel, weight 4.40 lb, measuring
16.53–25.19 in. in length.
Springfield SOCOM II—7.62 caliber, 16.25 in. barrel, weight 10.5 lb,
measuring 37.25 in. in length (Figure 3.2).

Another advantage of these shorter, high-power systems is that the decrease in length makes them easy to handle inside a vehicle, and they also can be more easily concealed.

SHOTGUNS

The "street howitzer," as it has been called by some, has a long history in law enforcement operations. A formidable weapon in the hands of even an average shooter, it has, however, somewhat limited use in protective work.

21

Given the spread of shot shells, it is perhaps best employed on static security posts where crowds of people are very limited. Issues with these weapon systems are size and ammunition characteristics. In the 1970s and 1980s, the Secret Service and State Department used shotguns with a shortened 14 in. long barrel and fitted with a pistol grip stock, resulting in a more manageable weapon. However, with the reduced barrel length, the shot pattern expands rapidly upon exiting, thus reducing the effective range.

While some departments may have access to cut-down shotguns, most still issue a full-size Remington 870 or perhaps a Benelli autoloader. The great length of some of these, coupled with their inherent ammunition capacity limits and the ballistic characteristics of buckshot, all reduce their viability in protective work. If shotguns are to be used, departments should seriously consider loading them with slugs for a more effective weapon.

SCOPES

When discussing scopes, it is not the "sniper"-style glass being referred to, but either ACOG or Aimpoint, "red dot" style. When mounted on an M-4, SOCOM 16, or similar weapon, the scope vastly increases the ability of the user to lock his aim onto the target prior to firing. In a sniper-based attack, this could be critical (see the Aimpoint red dot scope on the SOCOM II in Figure 3.2). Thought, however, needs to be given to whether the addition of such a device is offset by the increased lack of concealability. While many of those scopes are compact, when coupled with a weapon loaded with a magazine, it can be a handicap.

EDGED WEAPONS

A final weapon for teams to consider on a protective detail is the knife. A knife is a very versatile close-quarter battle (CQB) weapon that never jams, never needs to be reloaded, and can cause wounds that are immediately incapacitating (which cannot be said of firearms, which rarely perform the "one shot stop"). In addition to CQB uses, knifes are a tool that can assist in a variety of needs, such as cutting away a seat belt in the event of a major traffic collision. Which edged weapon should be carried? As with everything else on a discreet protective detail, concealability is a major factor, as are ease of access and rapid deployment (Figure 3.3).

22

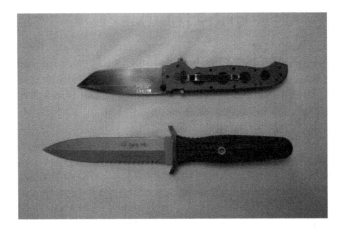

Figure 3.3 The two-edged weapons depicted in the photo are perhaps the ideal for a protective unit. The double-edged blade or "dagger" (bottom) is fixed and built for the sole purpose of CQB. The second, commonly referred to as a "combat folder," (top) is even more compact and easy to conceal, and yet when open and locked is a formidable weapon that could be used in CQB or for other cutting purposes.

The double-edged knife was built for one purpose only: fighting. Two early advocates and practitioners of the weapon were Captain William E. Fairbairn and Captain Eric A. Sykes, both of whom were British police officers in Shanghai, China, during the 1930s. These two men would later become famous for teaching covert agents to operate behind enemy lines during World War II. Many would later become the founding members of the Central Intelligence Agency. The reason the double-edged knife is so effective in CQB is that its design allows for slashing to be performed in any direction, while at the same time allowing deep "stabbing" attacks. Further, the cross guard prevents the hand from slipping onto the blade as a result of sweat or blood.

The combat folder, on the other hand, has a single edge and no cross guard. This means that the blade must be rotated in an attack. While obviously still useful in an attack situation, it is designed as more of a utility knife. Due consideration should be given to what knife to employ. A knife is only useful if it is available when it is needed. Therefore, for the protective detail member, the combat folder is perhaps the better of the two options as it is easily carried and fills a variety of needs. The choice is yours, but as with any equipment carried, it must be trained with to be effective.

OTHER EQUIPMENT

Depending on the situation—or rather, depending on the protected individual—the wearing of body armor needs to be considered. In most cases, the law enforcement team controls all elements of the operation, so instructing the protectee to wear body armor should be a requirement. Obviously, this may not be possible with department leadership and staff, beyond strongly encouraging its use.

Blasts, or, more correctly, ballistic blankets, are a potentially cost-effective means of providing ballistic protection for a principal, but with added flexibility. These blankets offer levels of ballistic protection up to level lllA. Ranging from 3 × 4 in. to 4 × 6 in. and bigger, they can weigh between 23 to 45 lb or more. Prices range around $3000 each. The benefit is that they can be kept inside a vehicle within reach of the protectee. In the event of an attack, it is simply a matter of the protectee pulling the blanket around himself or herself. While primarily geared toward explosives, their ballistic qualities make them ideal for protection from pistol and rifle rounds.

Another type of portable ballistic protection comes in the form of a briefcase. Upon an attack, the briefcase is opened and the ballistic "shield" unfolds to the size of 19 × 34 in. or larger. The most obvious use for such a device is while on foot moving between locations of cover. While most often employed by SWAT teams approaching a hostile location, they could easily be used to provide immediate ballistic protection to a protectee during an escape from an ambush.

MEDICAL CONSIDERATIONS

Should the unthinkable happen, and an ambush be sprung on a protective detail, there will be injuries. However, given that an attack is a fluid event, there will not be time to stop and render first aid or call for emergency medical services. Each and every team member will be his or her own "doc," as well as the protectee's doc, at least initially.

During an ambush, whether the team is in a vehicle or on foot, its priority is to engage the adversary while facilitating a rapid escape out of the kill zone. There is no time to assess breathing, stop bleeding, treating for shock, etc. In attacks on protected individuals, the vast majority of wounds will take the form of gunshots, followed by blast injuries. These injuries can vary widely in seriousness, from simple nicks and grazing wounds to sucking chest wounds, cut arteries, and even loss of limbs from explosive detonations.

Sucking chest wounds occur when a hole is punched through the chest cavity, thereby breaking the seal and collapsing the lungs. Lung collapse is one of the most lethal injuries, which impairs breathing; death will come quickly, and hence it must be treated immediately. The method of treatment is relatively easy, requiring the wound to be covered with a material that will assist in restoring the chest cavity's seal. The problem lies in having the material readily at hand in a compact traveling format.

Injuries to the major arteries of the human body, that is, the femoral, brachial, and carotid, whether from gunshot wounds or blast injuries, are life-threatening. As the blood spurts out with each beat of the heart, loss of consciousness will come in seconds, followed soon by death. Currently, there are several products on the market designed to immediately clot the blood, all of which are small, sterile, and self-contained.

Products such as Quik Clot are proved, but can be rather expensive at between $30 and $50 per package depending on the size and type ordered (Figure 3.4). Additionally, the shelf life of these items is around two years. Ideally, each team member should have two (as large caliber rounds have a tendency to have both entry and exit wounds), with a few more of these placed inside any medical bags that travel with a protective detail.

Depending on the nature of the gunshot or blast injury, a tourniquet may be the only means of stopping bleeding until arrival at a trauma center. Traditionally, a tourniquet in an emergency situation has taken the form of a belt, as they are often the most readily available. For a protective detail, this is a viable option; however, it can be problematic if an operator's weapon, magazines, and equipment are attached. The use of paddle holsters or shoulder holsters can remove this obstacle to a degree. Another option is a recently released tourniquet product that can be issued to each team member or kept in a medical bag (Figure 3.4).

If a decision is made to use a medical bag rather than each team member having their own (something that in the author's opinion should not occur), then one fully packed bag needs to be inside the passenger compartment of each vehicle. A medical bag in the trunk is useless for dealing with injuries sustained while escaping an attacking adversary. Finally, a problem with the medical-bag-only philosophy is, what happens if one is attacked while on foot? If injuries are sustained and the team cannot access the medical bag, what then?

Another option, one that is inexpensive to the point that it can be issued easily to each team member, is a sanitary napkin. These items are

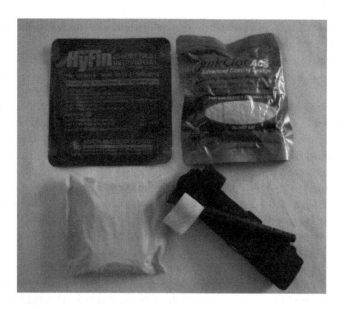

Figure 3.4 These essential first aid items easily fit inside a small bag that can be discreetly attached to a belt under a suit jacket. These items are (top, left) NyFin sealer for sucking chest wounds, (top, right) Quik Clot, (bottom, left) a sanitary napkin and (bottom, right) a tourniquet.

generally individually packed in a sealed and sterile wrapper, allowing them to easily be placed in a pocket. Their "normal" use is to stop the flow of blood. (Author's note: Its effectiveness for such use was confirmed by a former female team member. She stated that she had awakened one morning to discover that her sutures from her recent C-section had opened and that she was losing a tremendous amount of blood. She had her husband apply sanitary napkins to stem the flow of blood until she arrived at the hospital. Doctors later told her that the move probably saved her life.) The key point regarding these items is to acquire those with "super absorbency" as there can be no room for timidity on "flow" amounts, for men or women.

Finally, for decades the U.S. military has issued "dog tags" to each service member regardless of branch of service or rank. One of the key pieces of information provided, beyond the person's name, is their blood type. More recently, military troops have begun displaying their blood type on the outside of their uniforms. The simple reason is that with certain wounds, when seconds count, the correct blood type information being

DATE	June 4, 2010
NAME	John Doe
DATE OF BIRTH	3/14/1965
BLOOD TYPE	A-Neg
MEDICATION ALLERGIES	None known
CURRENT MEDICATIONS	None
MEDICAL CONDITIONS	None
EMERGENCY CONTACT	Jane Doe at 555-3845

FIGURE 3.5 A simple form such as this could make all the difference in those critical first minutes on arrival at a trauma center and should be filled out by everyone on the operation.

immediately known can make all the difference. The same technique should be adopted by a protective team.

Before any operation, it is a good idea to have each member of the team and the protectee complete a medical emergency form (Figure 3.5) providing information, such as blood type, known allergies to medications, and any medical conditions a doctor should be aware of in the event that the individual is unable to provide the information following an attack. These forms should be placed in an envelope and sealed by the owner. The envelope is then signed over the seal and given to the team leader to be held while the operation is on. Once the operation has been completed, the envelope is returned to the owner (a sample is provided in Appendix B, Medical Form).

VEHICLES

Vehicles used in protective details are a critical piece of equipment for a team. Unfortunately, with the vast majority of city and county agencies, the types of vehicles to select from are limited by fleet management. Often, they can limit the degree to which a vehicle can be modified for a team's intended use. Currently, the most prevalent vehicles consist of the Ford Crown Victoria, which for the 2010 model has an engine of between 224 HP to 250 HP (Interceptor package) for a vehicle that weighs over 4000 lb. Next is the Chevy Impala, with power ranging between 211 HP and 230 HP for vehicles weighing between 3500 to over 3600 lb. The Ford Taurus 2010 model has a power range of between 263 HP and 365 HP, but it weighs a staggering 4368 lb. More recently, the Dodge Charger has started to make its appearance in fleets; it has between 178 HP and 425 HP with a total weight between 3727 and 3800 lb.

What these vehicles have in common is that they are often readily identifiable as "government," which obviously defeats the covert nature of a detail. They also are very heavy, especially when you add between 300 and 800 lb of weight in the form of people and equipment. All of this will affect the overall performance of a vehicle during high-speed evasive maneuvers.

VEHICLE MAINTENANCE

Generally, fleet vehicles are maintained based on mileage and length of time between servicing. Short of any problems identified prior to the service date, it is possible that a vehicle on a protective detail would not be checked more than once every six months. Therefore, before a detail, the driver should inspect his or her vehicle regularly. This should consist of checking the oil, water, tires, and brakes, and looking for signs of tampering (brake lines cut, material put inside a gas tank, items stuffed up an exhaust pipe, lug nuts significantly loosened, etc.). This can easily be incorporated into the check for explosive devices on a vehicle.

Enhancements of fleet vehicles beyond lights and siren are probably restricted for the most part. However, two modifications that can probably be performed with likely minimal resistance are the tinting of windows and the installation of camber/strut bars. The use of tinted windows on vehicles is one of the easiest and cheapest upgrades for protective vehicles. The caveat is that all four side windows along with the rear should be tinted as dark as possible. This obviously provides a much darker interior, preventing team members and weapons from being visible, but more importantly, allows for the principal to be placed in a variety of locations. Using more than one vehicle of similar configuration increases the protectee placement possibilities (this is covered in detail in Chapter 8).

Camber or strut bars are another relatively quick and inexpensive upgrade. More often found on higher-performing sports cars, these bars are attached to the strut towers in the front of a vehicle and, in some, to the rear (Figure 3.6). The function of the bar is to prevent, or at least limit, the tilt of vehicle tires, called *camber*, that occurs during hard cornering. This will limit or prevent the body roll of the vehicle, thereby keeping more

Figure 3.6 More often found on high-end sports cars, strut bars are just as useful for protective sedans and are an easy bolt-on vehicle enhancement.

tire surface in contact with the driving surface. Without such a bar during hard cornering, the wheels on one side of the vehicle could break traction with the roadway, and the driver could lose control of the vehicle. The difference has to be felt to be believed; it does make a major difference. Given the advantages of taking as many corners as quickly as possible during an escape from an ambush, a protective detail should be provided every ounce of advantage that a vehicle can allow (Figure 3.6).

Two other modifications that can be beneficial are brake light kill switches and the relatively new technology, armored door inserts. Brake light kill switches are a trick that can easily be installed on vehicles with relatively little modification. While its use would be limited generally to nighttime transportation and then only when trying to evade hostile surveillance or attack, being able to disable the brake lights would allow a motorcade vehicle to hit the brakes hard prior to executing a sharp turn, leaving an adversary with no advance notice of the maneuver. It could make all the difference in making a successful escape. Armor inserts for doors are currently manufactured by Ford Motor Corp. for use in their Crown Victoria police sedan. While not cheap, they do provide an added measure of security that could make all the difference. However, even with this upgrade, windows are still the weak point and the area most adversaries will be focusing upon with their weapon fire.

MANUFACTURING ISSUES

Increasingly with modern vehicles, manufacturers are incorporating a variety of safety features in order to save lives in the event of a collision. Unfortunately, some of these "features" could prevent a protective detail from employing some evasive maneuvers used to escape an ambush. Additionally, some of these safety features are not generally advertised, so it is entirely possible for most owners, including fleet services, to be unaware of their existence.

Consider the following scenario: A two-vehicle motorcade is proceeding along a roadway when it is suddenly ambushed by a hostile vehicle intercept technique (vehicle rapidly pulls out in front and comes to a stop blocking any forward movement). As aggressive shooters begin to bail out of the intercepting car, the two protective drivers immediately come to a stop, throw their vehicle transmissions into reverse, hit the gas and execute perfect simultaneous reverse 180-degree turns. Almost immediately afterward, the engines of both cars shut down. The protective motorcade now finds itself in the unenviable position of having to fight its way out of their vehicles, and out of the ambush, on foot.

What caused these vehicles to shut down is a safety feature that has quietly been around for many years. In order to reduce the risk of vehicle fires resulting from a traffic collision, an application was developed and installed on some vehicles that automatically shuts down the fuel supply to an engine should a vehicle become involved in an accident. It also has been reported that if a vehicle travels beyond a certain degree off-center, the fuel supply could be shut down. With Ford vehicles, in particular, the device is known as an inertia fuel shut-off switch. When a sensor detects an accident, it shuts down the power to the fuel pump to prevent fuel from leaking out and perhaps causing a fire (a feature recently added to 2011 Volkswagen vehicles). It was found that General Motors vehicles, including Chevrolet (Impala, etc.), do not employ any sort of fuel shut safety feature. With Dodge vehicles, this feature engages only when the vehicle rolls over. Additionally, in some of these vehicles, the fuel system can only be reengaged by hitting a reset button, often located in the trunk of the vehicle. A team must check with the manufacturer of any vehicles they employ on protective operations to determine the presence of security features that could hinder their operations.

In some of the more "high-speed" driving schools, the topic of ramming vehicles to escape an ambush situation is discussed and taught. There are primarily three ways of using a vehicle to ram another. The most obvious is while driving in a forward motion, striking the adversary's vehicle in the rear portion of the vehicle around the trunk (the lightest part of a vehicle). The second is while reversing out of an ambush area and striking the adversary's vehicle with the rear end of the protective vehicle. (Caution: Another safety feature in some vehicles is a fuel shut-off following impacts near the gas tank.) The third method is the technique known by a number of names such as the Pursuit Intervention Technique, or the Precision Immobilization Technique, but more commonly referred to as the PIT maneuver.

The PIT technique uses the front sides of a vehicle near the front tires. By striking an adversary's vehicle around the area of its rear tires with the front sides of the protective vehicle will cause the adversary's vehicle to spin around (if conducted correctly, which requires practice). There is also a reverse PIT maneuver that is used if an adversary attempts to PIT your vehicle. The use of vehicles in ramming, or PITs, brings up the next major safety feature of modern vehicles that could handicap a protective team effecting an evasive maneuver.

If your vehicle is newer than mid-1980s, it most likely has airbags at least for the driver, and by the late 1980s, airbags were standard for driver and passenger. In the United States, it became an industry standard in 1998. Since the late 1990s, more and more vehicles are becoming equipped with side impact airbags. Airbags deploy when between 12 and 15 pounds of pressure is applied to the crash sensors located at the front or sides of a vehicle. Any impact detected by these sensors will cause the airbags to deploy at a speed of between 175 and 200 mph.

While designed for safety, they have caused some horrific injuries, and if nothing else, could stun the driver and passenger for several precious seconds. Injuries have included sunglasses forced into the skin of the face, skin removed from arms along the inside, etc. For a protective detail, these two consequences alone would effectively neutralize, or at a minimum delay for several critical seconds, a response from just about any operator. This poses a difficult dilemma that must be considered by a protective team, most likely in conjunction with fleet services and city or county attorneys. Should vehicles used in protective operations have the airbags disengaged, left as designed, or have a cutoff switch? Statistically, a team is more likely to be involved in a legitimate accidental traffic collision, where airbags would be of great benefit, than in a targeted ambush.

While a cut-off switch may be a viable option, it would have to be employed either before a protective motorcade detail or not at all because, in the heat of an attack, there would not be time to switch it on. If a protective team, however, decides to not have airbags in play on details, but the vehicles are used at other times, then the cut-off switch may be the best option. In instances where airbags are left operational, consideration should be given to placing the second operator in the backseat rather than the front passenger seat.

Case in point: On Tuesday, November 21, 2006, in Beirut, Lebanon, government minister Pierre Gemayel was driving his personally owned vehicle in the company of two protective operators, one of whom was seated in the backseat. As the three men were traveling, a vehicle directly in front of Gemayel's car suddenly applied the brakes, causing him to crash into the back of the vehicle with enough force to partially buckle the front hood. A second vehicle quickly blocked the rear, and, at the same time at least three men jumped out of the vehicles and open fired with automatic weapons, killing Gemayel and the protective detail member in the front seat.[2]

The majority of weapons, vehicles, and equipment discussed are already part of a department's inventory, or could be acquired with little investment. If a law enforcement protective function is to be provided, then those men and women need the tools to do the job.

ENDNOTES

1. McGovern, Glenn, *Targeted Violence: A Statistical and Tactical Analysis of Assassinations, Contract Killings, and Kidnappings*. (Boca Raton, FL: CRC Press, 2010).
2. Lebanese Christian Leader Killed, *BBC News*, Middle East, November 21, 2006, http://news.bbc.co.uk/2/hi/6169606.stm.

4

Training for the Adversary

When you have opposing forces facing each other with weapons and the intent to kill, it has all the elements of combat.

CSM Mel Wick
U.S. Army (Ret.)

The nature of protective operations most simply defined entails the pickup of a protectee or principal from a location and the transport of him or her to another location safely. This process is repeatedly conducted around the world without incident every day. However, the threat that a protective operation faces is one of the deadliest tactics in all of history, the ambush. The training required for a protective team, beyond its most basic movements to deal with such situations, is immediate-action drills designed to reduce the response time, and thereby the damage, incurred in the ambush. However, as in any of the combat arts, it is easy to get carried away with training. The goal should be to train realistically to deal with those known/potential adversaries in your area of operations. However, at the same time, a team needs to train to deal with the worst-case scenarios. The key is to find the happy medium so that a team can effectively handle a worst-case scenario, and the more mundane protective details.

Basic protective work training should include the concepts associated with motorcade operations and the various protective ring formations, along with site surveys and protective advance procedures. Much of the basic material has been covered in great detail in previous literature from CRC Press, the American Society for Industrial Security (ASIS), and others, and, therefore, will not be reviewed in this work. However, this information needs to be learned through practical training from a quality training organization, which all members should be required to attend. SWAT teams do not send just some of their members through a SWAT school, and neither should protective details.

Before delving into training for specific types of attack, it is necessary first to explain some of the principals of attack and counterattack, more specifically that of ambush and immediate action drills, and the nuances of both. It is only through a complete understanding of these concepts that an individual and team will be able to effectively train. The first concept then is that of the ambush.

Regardless of the type of the attack encountered by a protective detail, they all fall under the title of "ambush." In the United States Army Ranger Handbook (SH 21-76), it defines an ambush as "a surprise attack from a concealed position on a moving or temporarily halted target." It goes on to identify some of the key concepts to conducting a successful ambush, including:

- Coverage of the entire area of the kill zone with fire
- Use of existing or reinforcing obstacles to keep the enemy in the kill zone
- Assault through the kill zone
- Time the actions of elements to preclude loss of surprise

The ambush represents one of the oldest techniques in warfare because it works, which is precisely why it is taught and practiced by every military unit in the world as well as just about every terrorist organization. However, unlike in a war zone where opposing forces plan and prepare for conducting and responding to ambushes, for individuals and protective teams going about their daily business in towns and cities where such conflicts don't exist, the ambush is the last thing they would expect. While the surprise and violence of action in conducting an ambush is the same whether conducted in a war zone or a city street, there are differences in ambushes conducted in regions not experiencing a hostile conflict. It is these differences, as well as the basics of the ambush, with which protective details need to be intimately familiar.

In order to properly conduct an ambush, a hostile force requires information, such as the routines, routes, and movement patterns of their targeted victim and if there will be the presence of a protective detail. A potential attack site needs to be selected that offers the necessary cover for action (cover allowing the hostile force to pre-position in an area without raising third-party suspicions, such as from store owners, civilians, etc.), while they await the arrival of the target. The selected ambush site will also require a route of rapid escape after the attack. As such, all of this demands a fair amount of surveillance and reconnaissance to occur well before the attack. Much of this needs to be conducted by physical inspection (covered in detail in Chapter 9), hence the need for early identification of potential ambush sites by a protective advance (in Chapter 6).

The nature of the ambush is the perfect combination of two features: surprise and extreme violence of action. Successful ambushes employ these two traits, effectively and rapidly. The combination of these takes advantage of a factor of the human physiology. For protective teams to train effectively, it is vital they obtain a solid understanding of the affects.

PHYSIOLOGICAL/PERCEPTION CHANGES AND EFFECTS ON THE HUMAN BODY

An important aspect for all team members to understand is how reacting and responding to an attack will cause some dramatic changes to their bodies. While not everyone will experience and/or recall the events in the same way, the physiological changes will be similar. As Lt. Col. Dave Grossman (Ret.) and Loren W. Christensen explained in their seminal work *On Combat: The Psychology and Physiology of Deadly Conflict in War and in Peace*, when placed in high-stress situations, the human brain loses the ability to conduct fine and complex motor skills.

Anyone on the receiving end of an ambush will experience what Bruce Siddle has termed *combat stress*, "…the perception of an imminent threat of serious personal injury or death, of the stress of being tasked with the responsibility to protect another party from imminent serious injury or death, under conditions where response time is minimal."[1] This definition could almost be used to detail why the ambush is such an effective tactic. The effects of this combat stress are substantial, including tunnel vision, loss of fine and complex motor skills, loss of motor control, and auditory exclusion, all of which have a negative effect on the reaction and response time by the individual or group being attacked.

This stress is the result of the sympathetic nervous system or SNS, releasing a massive amount of hormones into the body in order to activate the "fight or flight" response. This release is automatic and is an evolutionary reflex. In studies, it has been discovered that the degree to which hormone release occurs can be controlled to a point. A low-level release occurs when a person knowingly goes into a hostile or dangerous confrontation, such as police carrying out search/arrest warrants and military units on raids. However, when the action is unanticipated, violent, and with little to no time to react, the "dump" is massive and immediate.[2]

This hormone/adrenaline can cause a person's heart rate to rocket from a comfortable 70 beats per minute to over 200 beats per minute (bpm) in less than one second. In tests on police officer subjects using only paintball guns, and knowing they could not be injured or killed, heartbeats of between 200 and 300 per minute were recorded. As the heart rate accelerates, a loss of abilities is experienced by the individual. At 115 bpm, fine motor skills or those that require eye–hand coordination, such as accurately aiming a weapon and maintaining trigger control—but also something as simple as the ability to release a seat belt—start to deteriorate.

At 155 bpm, complex motor skills start to deteriorate or those that involve a number of muscles requiring coordination and timing, such as getting into a shooting position, magazine changes, etc. At 175 bpm, tunnel vision and tunnel hearing starts to develop as well as a loss of depth perception and near vision. At above 175 bpm, the voiding of bladder and bowels can occur, and a person (depending upon his or her training, experience, and mental preparedness) may freeze, unable to take any action. However, the person's gross motor skills (running, charging, fighting, etc.) are at their optimum level.

In an ambush situation, as the first rounds start penetrating a vehicle and/or comrades, screaming, blood splattering, everyone will be frightened beyond all measure. The human body will automatically switch control of thinking from the forebrain to the midbrain, that is, reverting to the survival instincts of the primitive animal that we all are.[3] In addition to the effects of the heart rate on the central nervous system, the rate affects reaction times. There have been a number of studies on reaction times for police officers, all of which found that "reaction takes time."[4] In one of the studies of 1400 officers who *knew* they were being tested for speed, an average time for an officer to react to a visual stimulus of a threat was 0.73 seconds. The same study found that it took the same officers 2.84 seconds to draw a gun and double-tap a target.[5]

While it is difficult to know, with any degree of certainty, the average duration of a targeted attack, given that the ambush usually occurs at isolated locations and generally there is not someone standing with a stopwatch, they are known to be very rapid and extremely violent attacks. However, there have been two recent attacks that were captured on closed-circuit television (CCTV)—that of the 2007 attempted assassination of Senator David Figueroa in Mexico City and of an Italian mafia crime boss in Naples in 2009. In the nonscientific timing of these two hits, from the moment the weapon was drawn to the time when the assassin fled the scene, the times were 6 seconds and 8 seconds, respectively. In a videotaped police reenactment of the kidnapping of Aldo Moro in Italy, the entire attack (motorcade intercepted, all bodyguards killed, Moro forced into a nearby car, and all suspects depart the scene) lasted approximately 40 seconds.

Given the human body's "wiring" for dealing with high-stress moments, it is critical for a protective unit to be trained to respond through repetition. In studies of law enforcement shootings, many stated they had no conscious memory of their actions, rather they "responded automatically."[6] Therefore, a team should train in immediate action drills using high-stress, force-on-force training. It is only through this means that a team can have some reasonable chance of effectively responding to an attack automatically.

BASIC CONCEPTS

In training to respond to an ambush, there are some concepts that are more commonly associated with military operations and not usually taught to police officers. However, these concepts must be learned and understood by a protective team in order for them to be able to respond in the most effective manner possible.

Immediate Action Drills

Immediate action drills are tactics that have been developed and practiced to the point that a team can react decisively upon being attacked by an adversary. It permits the team to react to the threat without the need for verbal communication. The pattern of movement of immediate action drills, especially in regard to protective details, is complicated by the fact that responding to an attack requires team members to move within close proximity to one another with weapons drawn and firing. This close quarters battle, or CQB, is ironically considered an advanced combat skill by both military and police special operations units. It is regarded as advanced due to the increase in potential injury to team members if conducted haphazardly.

Protective details may have to function in close proximity to one another, as well as innocent civilians and within restrictive environments, such as inside of a vehicle, a hall, an elevator, etc. The nature of this action demands that teams have extensive training in CQB and in immediate reaction drills. This advanced training instilled over a period of time gives the operators the ability to scan for threats, keep the location of other team members and the protectee in mind, locate positions of cover, etc., all with little to no conscious thought. For this reason, the drills need to be based upon the KISS (Keep It Simple, Stupid) principle. Only by practicing these drills continuously, will the team obtain an increase in the overall proficiency.

Fire Superiority

Fire superiority means that one side is able to fire more rounds and/or more accurately than the adversary. Gaining fire superiority is more of an art form than science, in that it incorporates quality weapons, good weapon handling, and solid training as well as the advantageous use of cover. Obviously, this requires a fair amount of practice to develop to the level that protective teams should have and maintain. Used in a defensive mode, fire superiority or "cover fire" serves to disrupt the enemy and cause attrition as he starts to close with his target. One important factor in gaining fire superiority is fire discipline, for without it, you cannot maintain the other very long.

Anyone who has ever fired a magazine-fed weapon can attest to how quickly a magazine is emptied. When a weapon runs dry, it becomes useless beyond serving as a metal club until it is reloaded. If the weapon is used in an automatic function, the rate in which the average magazine of 30 rounds is emptied can be less than 2 or 3 seconds. In order to control this, the operator must consciously release the trigger of the weapon being fired in full automatic mode. This allows the operator time to readjust his aim, reevaluate the situation, and either reengage the target or move to another. Fire discipline can be the difference between successfully defending against an assault and being overrun. Fire all your ammunition in the first few seconds of a firefight, and you can bet the enemy will still have some left to finish you off. Fire discipline separates the professionals from the amateurs or, perhaps more appropriately, the living from the dead.

Breaking Contact

The immediate goal of anyone on the receiving end of an ambush is immediate evacuation out of the kill zone. If the adversary has properly planned the attack, this is much easier said than done. In the military, the general response to an ambush is to charge into and/or through the attacking force. In law enforcement, the general response is to drive through the kill zone. In protective operations, the response lies somewhere in the middle.

Known as a *retrograde movement* in military vernacular, it is perhaps better known as simply a retreat. It involves one person or team moving away from the threat to a position of cover. The best way to conduct such a tactical movement is by a technique known as the *bounding overwatch* or *leapfrogging.* This is performed by one person or team moving to a position of cover as another provides cover fire as needed, followed by the first team or person providing cover while the second moves, and so on. The goal is to keep the attacking force pinned down, preventing them from firing as the detail moves out of the area.

In many an ambush on motorcades, the adversary develops a method of stalling the vehicles within the kill zone. This allows the adversary to lock down the target long enough to pour down gunfire.

Case in point: On Saturday, April 24, 2010, at approximately 3 p.m. in Milenio, in the state of Michoacán, Mexico, Minerva Bautista, the Public Safety Secretary, was ambushed. The attack occurred as her three-vehicle motorcade was returning from having attended a regional fair. At some point along the route, a large truck trailer rapidly pulled in front of the motorcade and stopped, causing the motorcade to come to an abrupt halt. At roughly the same time, an estimated 20 gunmen open fired with automatic rifles and grenades, as well as a .50 caliber rifle. Four members of the detail were killed and another 10 people, including the Secretary, were wounded. The remaining members of the detail were able to fight off the attacking force and ultimately drive out of the ambush zone.[7]

Whether the intercept is accomplished by a vehicle or an improvised explosive device (IED), if the motorcade is unable to drive through or reverse out of the ambush zone, they must then exit or "deboard" their vehicles. Exiting a vehicle while under fire is a skill just like everything else in this line of work that must be developed. As always, start slowly and build up the skills. Position team members inside a vehicle as they would normally be on a transport. Assume the attack forces the team to exit out of a vehicle from one side or another (rehearse in both directions).

How can this be performed quickly and smoothly? Moving out of a vehicle while staying low, and getting into positions of cover to allow for the members to engage the threat, takes practice. Does everyone bail out at the same time or do one or more operators hold position to provide cover fire for the rest of the team? Only your team can make the final decision.

If another vehicle is available for escape, how does the team move to that vehicle? How do they enter and who enters? What happens to the rest of the team forced to stay in position and fight? Again, this is a matter for the team to give thought to and decide. Ultimately, these decisions should become part of the team's standard operating procedures.

Prolonged Engagements

Responding to an ambush brings us to another factor that needs consideration by the team before an attack ever occurs. Should a protective team find themselves in the unenviable position of being ambushed and having to fight their way out, there are several factors that must be considered. In these situations, when everyone is afraid, there may be a tendency to fire one's weapon in the direction of a threat without ever having a target. Each operator needs to remember they will only be able to stay in the fight and alive while they have ammunition and cover, and are not severely injured.

The attacking force, knowing an armed detail, is present, whether it is one officer or eight, is aware they will need to employ superior firepower to overcome any resistance and prevent any counter offensive. While prolonged engagements have occurred, they are, thankfully, relatively rare. However, none of us wants to be the statistic marking the first occurrence in the United States. One of the key factors in fighting through prolonged engagements is ammunition supply.

Ammunition Concerns

Generally speaking, most cops carry three magazines of between 8 and 15 rounds when on duty: one in their weapon and two spares in a pouch. Depending on the type of ammunition the weapon takes, the officer has anywhere from 25 to 46 rounds. Under normal conditions, that would be plenty, especially when most uniformed officers also have a shotgun or rifle if needed. However, in protective work, this may be nowhere near enough; adequate ammunition depends a lot on the number of personnel assigned to the detail, and the potential threat. In an ambush situation facing a determined, heavily armed adversary, and perhaps cut off from being able to rapidly withdraw from the kill zone, the team could easily run out. Protective teams, unlike SWAT teams, have no access to extra equipment, ammunition, etc. They are self-contained and will only have available that which they have brought with them.

By way of example, in training to respond to a real attack, I developed a training scenario, which was taken from the attacks perpetrated on Herr Schleyer by the RAF in Germany and Pierre Gemayel in Lebanon by Islamic extremists. In both of these attacks, a single vehicle with the protectee and a protective detail, consisting of a driver and one or more members, was blocked from the front and hit from behind to prevent escape. In the scenario, the protective member, seated in the back seat (refer to Chapter 8 for this positioning) and armed with a subgun, was to rapidly exit the vehicle and lie down, covering fire with controlled bursts on full auto and engaging two to three adversaries in front and two to three more in back. This cover fire was to allow the driver the time and cover necessary to grab the protectee, exit the vehicle, and bound to the nearest cover.

What we discovered was that, at our then operational load, the single protective member had only enough rounds to last between 30 and 45 seconds, including rapid magazine changes, before he ran dry and had to transition to his side arm (see Fire Superiority this chapter). As a result of this exercise, we had to reevaluate our operational load for our various weapon systems.

So, what should your operational ammo load be? Ultimately, that is a decision for the individual agency and, preferably, the team. It is also dependent upon the type of weaponry being deployed. If you were to be armed solely with a handgun, then you would want enough ammunition that you could comfortably carry. If you also carrying a subgun, then you might reduce your handgun ammunition in order to increase spare submachine gun magazines.

TYPES OF ATTACK TO TRAIN FOR

In order to properly "train for the adversary," the first requirement is identifying, to the extent possible, who the adversaries are and their preferred methods of operation. In some regions of the globe, this is easier to accomplish than others. For example, in Mexico, the adversary during the mid through late 2000s was the drug cartels. Their preferred method of attack was drive-by shootings, and their preferred victim was the ranking police official.[8] In Spain, over the past 30 years, the adversary has been the Euskadi Ta Askatasuna, or ETA (Basque Fatherland and Liberty), and their preferred victim of attack was the military officer. Their preferred method of attack has been shootings; however, explosives also were used in a large percentage of attacks.[9] The Tamil Tigers of Sri Lanka ruthlessly hunted their quarry using the suicide bomber.

Unfortunately, in most countries, the identification of potential adversaries is more difficult to determine. In those instances, it is incumbent upon protective details to identify groups that could present a threat in the future, should they decide to target a protected individual. Once these groups have been identified and an examination of their methods of operation has been conducted, the team can begin to train to respond to those types of attacks most likely to be encountered. In instances where there is no identified group or threat, the team should then focus its training on the most common form of attacks to be faced by a team. Some consideration could also be given to extremist groups linked to prominent cultures in the local region.

While the diverse population of the United States is one of our greatest strengths, it also brings with it inherent weaknesses. The vast majority of cultures are peaceful, but as with everything in life, there also are undesirable features. Examining the local culture base and countries of origins, extremist groups linked to a country, ethnicity, religious identity, etc., could provide a team with an indication of possible adversaries a team could face. Obviously, states boarding Mexico would have to closely monitor and analyze the tactics of the various drug cartels. In areas such as New York City and the San Francisco Bay Area, many more countries would need to be monitored.

Remember that the goal is for the team to train to deal with real-world situations, which this author is a strong proponent of (which led one colleague to state that they were "being trained to fight the Taliban," but at least they were prepared). Unfortunately, for those of us in the United States, the types of attacks that have occurred over the past 60 years have run the gamut from the lone gunman to vehicle-borne improvised explosive device (VBIED) attacks. Further, this is one of the great difficulties with protective operations; they have been carried out by a diverse group of individuals and organizations. This can then contribute to a general lack of specific knowledge of where the attack will most likely come from.

TRAINING THE TEAM

Teams need to train in all the environments in which they will operate. They need to train with the same equipment, as they will carry on a detail. This provides the individuals and the team as a whole with the knowledge of what works and what does not in situations such as moving in the rain or heat in the sweltering environments with body armor under a suit; holding an umbrella while wearing a raincoat and suddenly having to respond to an ambush; in cold environments, shooting with gloves on; and using flashlights while firing on hostile subjects. All this and more need to be practiced repeatedly.

Before beginning the training of a team, some consideration should to be made on how the team is to operate. How many cars and protective members will normally be fielded on a protective detail (this information needs to be closely restricted—see Chapter 7 for more information)? This generally would be from between one to three vehicles and two to eight protective members. While training needs to encompass all extremes, the initial focus should be on the levels determined most likely to be provided (all of which should be detailed in a team's standard operating procedures (SOPs)).

For this work, we will use a two-vehicle motorcade with four members with a single protectee as an example. While on foot, all five individuals are in a protective diamond formation within one to three feet of each other, give or take, and moving to or from a parked vehicle. If we factor in what Gavin De Becker stated in his book *Just 2 Seconds: Using Time and Space to Defeat Assassins*, most adversaries are within a range of less than 25 feet from their target at the time of the attack. What kind of situation are we presented with? We are left with what is termed a close quarter battle situation.

CLOSE-QUARTER BATTLE

A CQB, as it is more often referred to, is an advanced skill taught to police special weapons and tactics teams as well as military special forces. The reason is primarily due to the inherent danger of this type of combat, not only from adversaries, but also from fellow team members. It is characterized by engaging an adversary at very short ranges, often involving high-intensity shooting while within very close proximity to fellow operators as well as innocent civilians. As a result of this, operators must have superb weapon-handling skills.

In the event that a four-person protective detail is attacked, one team member will need to physically take control of the protectee. Depending on the nature and reaction of the protectee, this could effectively take that operator out of the fight, leaving three to deal with the threat. In reacting to the attack, the team members will have weapons drawn and perhaps be firing on the attacking force, all while attempting to break contact and move as a team with the protectee to a position of cover and safety. An added difficulty is that unlike in typical scenarios where CQB is employed, such as in hostage rescues, in an ambush situation, the team members will be moving in reverse. Thus, the potential for things to go wrong is enormous.

Therefore, team members need to train with each other in different-sized teams, with different members. Everyone needs the opportunity to learn how their fellow operators will act and move, how they hold their weapons, and how they move among each other without sweeping the barrel, that is, pointing it across a teammate or protectee. If using subguns and assault rifles, how to get them into the fight quickly; how to move while under fire and firing at the adversary. The team must learn to communicate with each other in the heat of the battle. When they are going to move to cover, or when they are out of ammo and need to reload; how to reload when under fire and/or while moving.

With CQB training, there is no other option but to start slow at the beginning and build up the teams' abilities. Start with a team of two on a range, but unarmed, with another team member acting as a protectee. Practice moving in the various diamond formations. Practice moving forward, backward, and horizontally as though attacked. Once the team has a good feel for the movements, incorporate plastic training weapons similar to what they may deploy with on an actual detail. Are the team members keeping fingers off triggers, lowering the barrels of the weapons when moving around the team, all while moving forward, backward, and horizontally? As the team develops, increase the size of the protective detail to four and six members.

When the team appears comfortable, move to Airsoft or Simunition weapons and repeat the drills as before. Incorporate paper targets in the immediate area for the team members to engage while moving as a team. After the team feels capable at this level and all questions and concerns have been addressed, begin the live fire portion. Begin very slowly when going live the first few times. As the team becomes more comfortable, the speed of the exercise can be increased, but even then only to the point that is safe. This process of training a protective detail in CQB tactics will be repeated with each new function in which the team trains. Fighting from inside of a vehicle, exiting a vehicle under fire while moving to cover, bounding overwatch techniques, etc., all exercises should follow a similar training process until they are fully understood and every team member has demonstrated proficiency.

GUNFIGHTING

The vast majority of attacks against an individual, whether they were by themselves or in the company of a protective detail, were perpetrated by one or two gunmen.[10] It, therefore, behooves a team to begin the training with this most common attack scenario. First of all, the standard minimum number of law enforcement officers providing protection on a detail should be two; however, for whatever the reason, there are times when this is not feasible. There have been a large number of attacks in which the protectee was attacked and killed while in the company of a single protective member who was also the driver. If a department foresees the use of a single operator, then scenarios should be developed and practiced.

Case in point: On the afternoon of Wednesday, October 31, 2007, Mexican Senator David Figueroa survived an ambush by a lone gunman outside of the World Trade Center building in Mexico City. The attack occurred as Figueroa was preparing to enter his vehicle. He had just arrived on the passenger side of the car, while his driver/bodyguard was approaching the driver-side door. The lone gunman, wearing a suit, approached the senator from the same direction he had just come from, and in fact yelled, "Congressman!" This caused Senator Figueroa to look and recognize a gun being pointed in his direction. The assassin opened fire at the same time as the senator took cover behind the car. The gunman then ran toward the guard and pulled the trigger; however, the weapon malfunctioned and the gunman fled the scene.[11]

As many of these attacks are staged while entering a vehicle, time should be spent training to respond to just such a scenario.

Case in point: On Wednesday, September 13, 2006, at approximately 9 p.m. in Moscow, outside of a local sports stadium, Andrei Kozlov, the first deputy chairman of Russia's Central Bank and his driver/bodyguard Alexander Semynov were ambushed and killed. The attack occurred as Kozlov and Semynov were in the process of placing their sports equipment into the trunk of Kozlov's Mercedes after a bank employee soccer game that was habitually held every Wednesday. Two men were apparently waiting nearby and rapidly approached with pistols drawn, opening fire and killing both men. The two assassins then fled the scene in a vehicle waiting nearby.[12]

This type of training is straight gun fighting, right out of some Old West movie. Can the driver/operator draw and fire his weapon faster and more accurately than the adversary can draw and fire his at the protectee? Speed and accuracy are the name of this game. The use of Airsoft- or Simunition-type weapons allow for this training to be as absolutely real as possible. The practice drills should also be performed with the nuances of protective life, such as holding an umbrella and wearing a trench coat, entering or exiting a vehicle, etc.

Another form of attack that has seen some use, with lethal results, is what I have termed the *reverse.* In this style of attack, the assassin approaches the individual and/or protective detail head on and passes them. Upon reaching some predetermined distance, the assassin then turns, pulls out a weapon, and engages the target and/or protective team. This style of attack takes advantage of the difficulties in maintaining vigilance over what is occurring from behind. It also takes advantage of the potential skills-level deficiency of a protective team—namely, if detected, it requires a protective member to yell out the contact and location, while drawing his or her firearm and turning 90° to a full 180° to engage the target (a skill that is not often trained in by regular law enforcement and security officers).

Case in point: On Monday, May 6, 2002, in Hilversum, Netherlands, Wilhelmus "Pim" Fortuyn, a far-right politician, was assassinated. The attack occurred as he was walking toward his car after having just finished a radio talk show interview. While in the company of several other individuals in the parking lot, heading toward his chauffeured vehicle, he was passed by a single man, the assassin. This man after taking approximately five steps past his target turned and with a concealed 9 mm pistol, fired six rounds, five of which struck Fortuyn. The killer then fled the scene as Fortuyn died.[13]

This effective method of attack can be best trained for by using force-on-force training with Airsoft or Simunition weapons. The use of role players and moving through an area in various diamond protective rings will force the team to monitor a whole host of potential threats from numerous angles. This training will allow the team to learn to identify the furtive movements that an assassin may display, indicating he or she is preparing to attack. When using live weapons, consider implementing "El

Presidente" exercise. The drill begins with the operator facing away from three targets. On command, the operator pivots and double taps each target followed by a reload.

COUNTER SNIPER

Historically, most sniper-based ambushes have involved a single shooter/team at a distance of between 50 and 400 yards. The problem is that if the sniper is good or just lucky, the first you will know you are under attack is from the "pink mist" as your principal falls from the high-velocity bullet injury. It, therefore, is to a team's advantage to be very familiar with their normal area of operations (AO). Given the law enforcement environment, these locations are most likely going to be the office, courthouse, and residence. With the exception of the residence, areas around the office and frequented locations, like a court, should have already been surveyed for potential sniper nests. This survey should include the known distances between these nest possibilities and target points.

As a result of popular fiction, when a person thinks of a sniper in the urban setting, odds are they would imagine the man on the roof. While this position on high ground certainly has its benefits as has been demonstrated throughout history, it is not always the case. A relatively new method of employment for the sniper has been the mobile platform, generally consisting of a car or SUV modified to allow a person armed with a rifle to fire out the back of the vehicle. Perhaps first brought to worldwide attention after the Washington, D. C. beltway serial shootings, the extremists in Iraq during the 2002–2010 war began employing this tactic. Given the low positioning of the shooter, only two to four feet off the ground, its use is limited. However, under the right conditions, it could prove very effective as the sound would be muffled and the natural tendency when dealing with a perceived sniper is to look up.

Case in point: On Wednesday, June 12, 1963, during the early morning hours in Jackson, Mississippi, civil rights activist Medgar Evers was assassinated. The attack occurred as he was returning to his residence from his work with the NAACP. Unknown to him, in the dense vegetation across the street, not more than 50 meters distant lay his assassin, Byron De La Beckwith, armed with a British Enfield 30.06-caliber rifle with a telescopic scope. De La Beckwith had lain in wait for some four hours for Evers to arrive. As his victim exited his vehicle, De La Beckwith raised the rifle and lined up the crosshairs on Evers' back. As Evers approached his front doorway, De La Beckwith pulled the trigger a single time. The round penetrated Evers' body, continued through him and the front door, and came to a rest in the kitchen where Evers' family waited for his arrival. Evers fell and began crawling to the front door, which at the sound of the gunfire, had been opened by his wife. Evers was able to get through the door into his home but later died of his wound. De La Beckwith was able to calmly and quietly move out of the area.[14]

Whether a hostile organization will field a trained sniper unit or not is of little initial importance. Anyone with a moderate amount of shooting experience, especially hunters, could pick up a rifle and successfully engage targets within 100 to 200 yards. Given the nature of the urban/ suburban layout, most potential sniper concealments would fall within 50 to 200 meters. Whether the sniper is on a rooftop or inside a structure, what is ultimately visible? Most likely, a head and weapon, but certainly not a full-size human target. Therefore, you need to train for that.

First, you should obtain the distances around the offices and frequented locations where you know the team will work frequently (i.e., the office, courthouse, jails, etc.) and possible sniper positions. This can be found using a range finder that most SWAT team snipers have access to. Short of that, the use of Google Earth's distance measuring tool can provide a close estimate of range. Odds are the ranges will be within 100 meters or less, including changes resulting from elevation. The next issue is what weapon systems does the team have access to? If all you have is handguns and shotguns, you are severely limited in the level of protection you can provide. Hopefully, if providing a protective service, you have access to submachine guns and assault rifles (see Chapter 2). All of the assault rifles and a good number of subguns will be able to effectively deal with threats out to the 100-meter range.

The best way to train for the sniper threat is to recreate the elements of what will be faced. Obviously engaging elevated targets is very difficult to recreate, but if access to a range provides that opportunity, by all means it should be practiced. For most teams using the traditional flat range, mark out the distances common around your AO, and set up 10-in. diameter steel plates on a stand instead of the more common silhouette targets. Tell the team members what the distance is, but more importantly, that it is the same between the locations in the AO, such as a courthouse entrance and the stacked parking structure across the street.

Have the team engage the steel beginning with the prone position. Then move to the kneeling position, later adding cover, such as a vehicle. Include standing if there is cover for an operative to stand and engage a threat in the AO, such as a large tree trunk or column. Start slowly, but as the team gets better, practice rapidly getting the weapon in play, on target, and shots away as though being ambushed. This process will give the team the knowledge and confidence to deal with a sniper threat in an area where the team works regularly.

Fortunately, the use of rifles in a sniper-type attack is relatively rare in the United States. In the documented cases where it was used in a targeted attack, it was in the hands of a domestic extremist group rather than a criminal gang or organization. Unfortunately, many of these extremists that have carried out sniper-style attacks, and those that would consider it are generally very familiar with the weapon and will have practiced to some extent in precision shot placement. This means that a protective detail, at least in the United States, facing a sniper attack is, in all odds, facing a trained and dangerous adversary who knows tactics and the limits and abilities of the weapon system.

EDGED-WEAPON ATTACK

Targeted attacks by assassins armed with an edged weapon are rare, having been documented in only 24 attacks worldwide in the past 60 years. However, in nine of the attacks, a protective detail of some form was present at the time. The difficulty with defending against the knife attack is in the way it is designed to be used. It is perhaps the ultimate stealth attack weapon. It is easily hidden right up to the point of attack, whereupon it is rapidly deployed at extremely close quarters. Unlike attacks by firearms, edged weapons can produce multiple injuries that can be fatal in seconds, even before a protective team member can draw a weapon.

Therefore, training in defending against edged-weapon attacks should be a part of the repertoire of every competently trained protective team. Through the use of rubber or plastic training knives, such as Airsoft or Simunition weapons, it is possible to replicate a knife attack with the highest level of realism, speed, and stress. The best way to begin is by providing the team with training in the basics of knife fighting and the angles of attack. Understanding how knives can be used to inflict wounds to specific targets will enable them to better appreciate some of the defenses. Using rubber knives edged with red lipstick or a similar material, teams can practice going one-on-one in a knife fight (Figure 4.1). Lasting only a minute or two, what injuries were received by the two "fighters" and, more important, which ones are superficial and which ones are life threatening? There is no better way to show the reality of a knife attack.

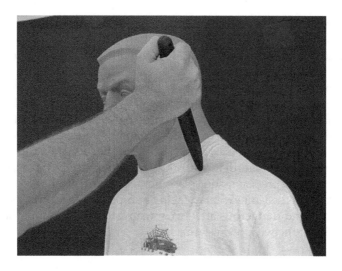

Figure 4.1 The use of a rubber practice knife, which could be rimmed with red lipstick, against a body opponent bag (BOB) at the area of the carotid artery.

The next stage is to bring realism of responding to a knife attack with a firearm, either pistol, subgun, or assault rifle. Again, using the Airsoft weapons and a rubber knife, practice should be conducted with assassins attacking from distances of 25 feet, 10 feet, and 2 feet. Initially, require the protective operator to remain stationary while responding to the attacking assassin. Next, require the operator to retreat backwards while responding to the attacking assassin. Finally, allow the operator to move laterally to the attacking assassin. It is through this method that the operators will obtain the clearest understanding of the benefits of moving laterally and forcing the assassins to change their angle of attack, providing more time to draw and fire a weapon.

From here the training should evolve to include team responses to edged-weapon attacks. Using the same distances as used in the one-on-one attack training, the team will learn the best methods of dealing with such ambushes. In extreme close-quarter attacks by edged weapons, operators must realize that in these instances the likelihood of their being able to draw and fire a weapon before they or their protectee is severely injured or killed is exceedingly unlikely. This, then, requires going hands-on with the assassin, an extremely dangerous prospect for an operator. The goal should be to distract the assassin while preventing him from delivering lethal wounds to the operator, taking him on while giving a second operator the time to draw a weapon and neutralize the threat. This can only be learned through direct force-on-force training and should be strongly considered by any protective detail.

COUNTER BOOBY TRAP

Between January 1950 and November 2010, there were a total of 40 targeted attacks found to have been perpetrated by way of a booby trap device. In the United States during the same time period, a total of five booby trap attacks were committed.[15] The very nature of these attacks circumvents a response from any tactical team in the world. The only way to counter such an attack is to detect the device prior to its detonation. Generally, an adversary employing such a tactic is looking to kill or harm a single individual and, therefore, will tend to focus the placement of the device on the believed position of this person. Of course, before this can be done, the adversary must first gain access to the target vehicle.

Ideally, all vehicles should be secured in a location that prevents easy access when left over night and/or for extended periods of time. Unfortunately, the level of security provided to law enforcement and their vehicles varies widely. It can range from secured, alarmed, underground parking to the more common flat, outside lot surrounding the department, perhaps with CCTV, to the worst-case off-site parking with little to no security, no CCTV, and perhaps not even lighting. In some instances, the vehicles to be used are assigned to individual officers as take-home vehicles. This increases the potential issues over the various levels of security available from secured garages to carports to parking on the street. Depending on the type of vehicle targeted and the type of explosive device, the adversary may need only seconds to secure a device on a vehicle. Then, it is just a matter of waiting for the right time to trigger it.

Herein lies another of the benefits of shifting the seating location of the protectee around in a vehicle and motorcade. The vast majority of booby trap devices contain a relatively limited amount of explosive (in terms of weight and power), as it is meant to be compact and placed under or right near where the target will be. If the adversary is not positive where in the vehicle the target may sit, they may be forced to employ a larger device to ensure the entire vehicle is destroyed, thereby limiting the places it can be attached and increasing the amount of time necessary to be spent on installation. If the possibility exists that the target will be seated in more than one vehicle, the adversary either deploys more than one device (which has never been recorded in the author's research, as having occurred) or more likely defers to a different method of attack.

Regardless of the level of security vehicles are afforded, if it is to be used in a protective detail and has been left unattended/unsecured for any duration (even if for just 30 to 60 seconds), it needs to be searched. While some vehicles searches can be extensive, generally that is not required. If, however, the amount of security of a vehicle to be used in a protective detail is such that anyone could have tampered with it for several hours with little chance of detection (i.e., obtaining access to the engine and/ or interior), then a very thorough search needs to be performed on that vehicle prior to its use.

Explosive devices must have three components in order to properly function: an energetic material (explosive), a power source, and a triggering device. Officers should keep this in mind when examining a vehicle for booby traps. While some devices may have their own power supply, others may tap into a ready supply from the vehicle. The devices can range from a crude pipe bomb with a timer to a couple pounds of plastic explosive wired into the engine compartment. Regardless, the size of the device will generally be small (approximately 4 in. in width and 10 in. in length, give or take).

The complete search of the average vehicle will take a considerable amount of time to perform effectively, safely, and correctly. The best way to start is by simply walking the complete circumference of the car. Beginning with the bodywork, look for fingerprints, disturbed dust, and new scratches such as from tools. Spend some time examining all exterior lighting (including the more modern ones inserted in the side-view mirrors). Look at the screws of the lens covers for signs of recent activity. Are there wires protruding from the light into or out of the vehicle?

Next, move to the tires and inside the fender wells. Again, look at the screws or "poppers" that hold it in place. These by their nature are filthy and will easily show signs of being disturbed. Look and feel up under the front and rear bumpers. This includes the spare tire if positioned under the trunk. Examine the access point to the gas tank for any foreign items. Look on the ground around and under the vehicle for bits of wire, electrical tape, plastic ties, etc. Finally, the undercarriage of the vehicle needs to be examined. This should be accomplished by lying down and using a flashlight, examine both visually and by gentle touch for any foreign items. Include a check of the exhaust pipe and muffler.

Once satisfied with the exterior, you move to the interior. Begin by examining all aspects of the interior via the windows. More specifically, examine the right (passenger) side of the interior via the left-side (driver) windows and vice versa. As before, look for any signs of the unusual or suspicious exposed wires, anything unusual along the dashboard, etc. With modern keyless entry, unlock the doors by remote and preferably from a position of cover. (*Note*: On most alarms, the remote unlocking of the vehicle also causes most of the exterior lighting to function.) If doors can also be opened by remote, then do so.

Slowly open the doors while visually inspecting and physically feeling along the edges. One school of thought is to affix a long rope to the exterior door handle and pull it open from a relatively safe distance away. However, for most modern doors, this is no longer an option. Once all four doors are open, then continue the visual and tactile search under the dash and all seats front and back. When satisfied, open the trunk. As with the doors, slowly open the trunk, feeling along the edges until it is completely open. Check along the backsides of the seats and the spare tire.

Finally, you will reach the engine compartment. Prior to popping the hood, attempt to gain a visual through the front grill. Pop the hood and slowly raise it to its full upright position. Carefully and patiently examine the engine compartment. Pay close attention to the battery and coil as they provide a ready power supply. Follow all wires and hoses, looking for signs of disturbance, newly applied black electrical tape, tubing, or old electrical tape and tubing with clean spots, etc. Once satisfied, start the car and proceed.

In those cases where the adversary is not known to or is not suspected of employing an explosive-based booby trap attack, and the vehicles have been relatively secure, a less thorough search can be conducted. Here, again, the search needs to be focused on those areas where a protectee could be expected to sit. Obviously, this would entail searching the undercarriage of the vehicle around the passenger seating and the wheel wells of the vehicle that abut the passenger seating as well as the engine compartment along the firewall (the author has witnessed individuals that can quickly and easily get into a vehicle engine compartment, install a device, shut the hood, and walk away, all in less than two minutes). When checking the undercarriage of a vehicle, mirrors can and should be used along with a flashlight. However, it will require the examiner to get a bit dirty to be able to check it well enough to confirm that no explosive device has been attached (Figure 4.2).

When searching, keep in mind the areas that can be quickly accessed by an adversary to attach a device. If the vehicle sits relatively low to the

Figure 4.2 Examine the engine compartment, focusing on the areas along the firewall.

ground, then as long as it was not elevated in such a fashion as to expose more of the undercarriage, the adversary will only be able to reach so far under the vehicle. If the vehicle is equipped with a covering of the undercarriage, then short of perhaps cutting a hole in the material, the adversary will need to locate another area in which to cache the explosive device.

In most vehicles, inside of the wheel wells is a covering that is either screwed into place or affixed with a plastic snap-type device. Most of these areas are very filthy with road grime, which is to your advantage. Are their fingerprints or signs it was wiped down? Are there some loose or missing screws, etc.? Basically, are there any signs or indications it has recently been tampered with? Signs that a vehicle may have been tampered with in order to cause a malfunction (i.e., the proverbial cutting of the break line) are more likely to be detected (Figure 4.3 and Figure 4.4) when the examiner is familiar with what the vehicle looks like under normal operation.

While it is not known if booby trap devices used in past targeted attacks employed any sort of antidisturbance triggers, you can never be sure. Additionally, depending on where the vehicle is located, if an adversary is watching the search and believes the device may have been located, he may decide to detonate it and take one life rather

Figure 4.3 Examine the trunk area—again, the area closest to the passenger compartment.

Figure 4.4 The wheel well area that could be used to place and conceal an improvised explosive device.

than have it disarmed. As any bomb technician in the world will tell you, whenever an improvised explosive device is encountered, leave it alone, evacuate the immediate area, and call for an explosive ordinance disposal team (EOD).

Modern encapsulated undercarriages—known in the industry as vehicle paneling, belly pan, or underpaneling—and carbon fiber vehicle body construction are becoming more prevalent; these have had a preventative affect against booby trap devices. The encapsulation, generally constructed of a plastic and/or fiberglass material, is meant to protect a vehicle's undercarriage from being damaged by road debris. An added benefit to this encapsulation is preventing easy installation of an explosive device. Further, the increasing use of carbon fiber material and plastics on the body construction limits the use of magnetic devices, thereby preventing easy slap on of an IED.

In training teams to search vehicles, as with most other protective detail training, a hands-on approach is needed. You can only learn to properly search a vehicle by doing it. A good method for this is to park several vehicles, preferably ones that the team will use on operations, in an isolated area (to prevent OPSEC [operations security] compromise). Have a variety of fake devices (clearly mark these as "inert") consisting of PVC and/or steel pipes with caps on only one end or a pound of modeling clay to simulate C-4 explosives (Figure 4.5).

When coupled with some wires, an old cell phone, etc., it will be readily identifiable as "suspicious." Contact your local EOD personnel for assistance as needed.

Have three team members place the devices on the vehicles. One car is completely secured with the alarm on. Another has a window partially down, allowing access to the door lock, and the other is left completely unsecured. The three "bombers" will gain valuable experience in the difficulties involved in concealing and placing a device, which will later assist them when they are having to search a vehicle prior to use. Once the devices are placed, the rest of the team should go through the process as previously explained to locate the devices. (*Note*: It should be constantly reinforced to the team that on finding a suspicious device, they need to detail as much information about the device, evacuate, and contact the local EOD team). Switch up the "bombers," so all on the team get the experience. Do not set any rules, but let them be realistically creative in order for the team to obtain the most benefit. Finally, remind all that even when one is found, the rest of the vehicle still needs to be searched when the EOD arrives.

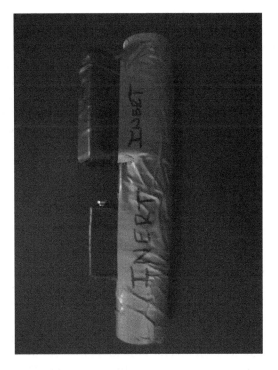

Figure 4.5 Example of a simple and common device that can be used in training, but, more importantly, it is clearly marked as "inert" and easy to confirm that it is not a real device.

Case in point: On Friday, June 19, 2009, at approximately 9 p.m. in an apartment complex parking lot just outside of San Sebastian, Spain, Eduardo Pueyes Garcia was assassinated by members of the ETA. Garcia, who was a police officer and supervisor of a police intelligence unit, had just gotten into his vehicle and was in the process of reversing out of the parking space when an IED booby trap device concealed on his car detonated. The device, which was believed to have been command detonated (meaning someone had watched from a distance and triggered the device remotely at the correct time), was found to have been placed near the gas tank and consisted of between 1.5 and 2 kilos of explosive material.[16]

COUNTER SWARMING

The swarming technique has been used with great success all around the world. It is especially effective on vehicles traveling on a tight urban street.

It allows a hostile force to quickly overwhelm a protective detail, trapping them inside their vehicle with little opportunity to move and engage the threat. The attacks on Aldo Moro on March 16, 1978, in Italy by members of the Red Brigades is a perfect example of the use of the swarm attack, as is the Red Army Faction (RAF) targeted attack on Hans Martin Schleyer on September 5, 1977. The technique is characterized by an adversarial force attacking a target from multiple angles. It has often been employed in conjunction with vehicle intercept attacks. For the protective team, the problem becomes being trapped inside of a vehicle (essentially one big death trap) while being attacked from two or more directions, thereby preventing escape from the vehicle. Hence, all armed protective teams must learn to engage threats from the confines of a vehicle.

SHOOTING FROM A VEHICLE

Given that a large percentage of targeted attacks occur in a drive-by fashion, teams need to train to respond to such a threat from inside of a vehicle. It is a skill that, while hopefully will never be used, needs to be trained and practiced by any law enforcement protective outfit as it presents a multitude of issues. Things that need to be considered first and foremost is what weapon systems in inventory lend themselves to being effectively used inside the confines of a vehicle? Obviously, a pistol is the easiest of all to use given their small size. Next would be the subgun, especially those that have a collapsible or folding stock. These types of stocks allow for the weapons to be fired with one hand in a relatively controlled fashion. Consider the opening scene in the movie *Quantum of Solace*, when James Bond fires a short burst from an H&K UMP 9 mm one handed with the stock folded closed. Granted it is Hollywood but, with that weapon system and some practice, it could easily be replicated by any operator.

If you have never practiced shooting from within a vehicle and you run protective operations, you need to start. The confines of a vehicle are extremely restrictive and in an ambush situation should be considered as a kill zone. If your adversary has planned correctly and your vehicle is prevented from driving through the ambush point and your vehicles are not armored, then the rounds, whether a 9 mm or a 7.62, will be able to easily penetrate into the interior. You have only a second or two in which to react to the ambush.

Of course, in an attack situation, rolling down a window is not a concern, and operators should engage threats as they present themselves.

Teams may have to rake the windows of glass in order to engage off angle targets. In training situations, this option is not usually available, so one of the first problems to understand is how far do the rear passenger windows roll down? For child safety reasons, often times these windows roll down only half to three quarters. This obviously can severely limit the ability of an operator to get into position in order to engage a threat.

With almost 50 percent of targeted attacks occurring while a target is traveling in a vehicle,[17] a team must train to fight from inside of a vehicle. The first part of this is to practice using a vehicle that will be used in an operation. It is of no use to train in a large roomy sport utility vehicle, if only sedans are used on details. The confines of a vehicle present a number of problems that all teams need to have identified and, more importantly, developed methods of working around and within it. Rear passenger windows that do not open fully, shooting weak handed, without sights on a moving target all while moving, keeping the finger off the trigger until ready to fire. Most importantly, manipulation of a weapon, without sweeping the business end of a weapon across a partner's body.

One of the first issues a team will realize is the limitation of some weapon systems. Inside a car is the realm of the submachine gun, assault rifles with collapsible stocks, such as the M-4 and, of course, the handgun. While a full-size rifle or shotgun could be used, they will be difficult to get into the fight and, in an ambush situation where every second counts, the last thing a team member wants is to struggle to get a weapon online.

Another issue is training to shoot a weapon on a weak side. Many officers have no doubt practiced weak-hand shooting with a handgun, but what of the subgun or rifle? A team needs to practice this. If a shotgun is to be employed (something the author feels should only be used for static security), it should be loaded with slugs given the tight quarters of this type of battle. However, try shooting a shotgun loaded with slug, weak handed, and without a firm stock weld into the shoulder.

Should you sling the weapon in case an operator is hit, thereby preventing the loss of the weapon by falling out of the vehicle? Can you deploy it inside with it slung? How will magazines be changed? Depending on the determined combat load, will you have a spare magazine and where will it be located? How fast can weapons be brought to bear; sidearms from a holstered and seat-belted starting position? Long guns (never cased), how are they to be positioned safely inside and how fast can they be brought to bear? What about the driver? In Northern Ireland during the "Troubles," the British Army unit known as Detachment 14, or "Det. 14," positioned a holster near the driver in which sat a Browning Hi-Power 9 mm pistol with a 20 round magazine.[18] Is that something a team wants to do? If so, it needs to be positioned and practiced in drawing and firing.

As with all training, start slow and build up a solid base. Position a vehicle on a range and have the team members positioned in different areas of the vehicle practice drawing and firing at targets in front and the sides. Switch the vehicle around, operators engage targets at the rear, and so on. When and if possible, it would be ideal for a team to have an opportunity to shoot through a side and rear windows. What happens to the trajectory of the first few rounds? Is the visibility of the target obscured by the shattered safety glass? Will it need to be raked clear? Are there glass blowback hazards? A team needs to know this and plan for it.

MOTORCYCLE-BASED ATTACKS

Targeted attacks involving the use of motorcycles have become increasingly popular around the world. Groups as diverse as Al Qaida, Colombian drug cartels, the various Italian mafia organizations, Germany's Red Army Faction, and many more have all employed motorcycle-bound hit teams with often lethal results. In fact, as recently as 2009, a Los Zetas training camp was discovered in which the focus of the training was on motorcycle hit teams.[19] It, therefore, behooves a team to train for responding to this style of attack.

Motorcycles present an interesting problem for protective teams primarily due to their mobility. They are characterized as highly maneuverable, capable of splitting lanes, traveling on sidewalks, rapid acceleration, and able to allow a second-armed team member to either fire from a seated position or quickly step off and close in on a target. Ambush locations in which a motorcycle would obviously be ideal are on narrow restrictive streets and/or areas of traffic congestion.

Another difficulty is the commonness of motorcycles with one or two riders in full protective gear. Without showing any overt signs of hostility, the motorcycle team could be alongside of a motorcade before anyone ever sees a weapon. If that weapon is a fully automatic submachine gun capable of firing 600 rounds per minute, a 30-round magazine will be emptied into the vehicles interior before anyone can react.

Because the vast majority of known motorcycle-based attacks have used a two-rider system,[20] that should act as an immediate alert when detected by a team. Every operator should be aware and ready to engage the threat if needed. If determined to be an attacking motorcycle team, ideally the driver of said motorcycle should be engaged immediately. First and foremost, if the driver is hit, the bike ceases to function. Secondly, the driver blocks most of the view of the shooter. However, as with a sniper threat, only a limited amount of the driver's body will be visible behind the handlebars, gas tank, and wind shield. This needs to be considered when engaging motorcycle practice targets on a range.

Finally, engaging a motorcycle hit team coming up from behind puts any protective member at a difficult angle to shoot. Shooting out the side windows back toward the threat could prevent the effective use of sights or require a shooter to use his weapon offhand. The other possibility, and probably the most effective, is to shoot through the rear window. Even then, if the attack is during rush hour or periods of traffic congestion, operators cannot just blast away through a window without regard for innocent civilian drivers. A team needs to think and plan its response for just such a scenario.

TRAUMA RESPONSE

An important aspect of training for the adversary is dealing with a medical emergency. Just as military units have long recognized the need and more and more SWAT teams adopt the Medic into their fold, so too must a protective team. Most police officers receive some level of training in basic first aid, generally encompassing CPR, treating for shock, choking, and stopping blood loss. This is sensible as it is predominately what police officers and security can expect to have to deal with on the street while awaiting the arrival of emergency medical technicians (EMT) or paramedics.

For protective teams, the level of medical training needs to be substantially expanded to deal with the potentially grave injuries resulting from gunshots and explosive blasts. In a worst-case scenario, the protected individual, as well as team members, could very likely sustain serious bodily injuries, including arterial bleeds from gunshots, amputated limbs from explosive blasts, and sucking chest wounds resulting from a bullet piercing the chest cavity and lung, causing deflation.

Depending on the nature of the attack, team members may be forced to provide their own trauma care, from applying compression bandages (to severe gunshot injuries), tourniquets, and even chest seals. Further, there could easily be a delay in getting oneself or an injured protectee to a trauma facility. According to Col. Ronald Bellamy, the U.S. Army Medical Chief of the Water Reed Medical Center, 90 percent of combat wound fatalities died on the battlefield before reaching a medical treatment facility. As such, it is strongly suggested that protective units seek out hands-on training from SWAT and/or military medics in dealing with what can only be termed "battlefield injuries."

As part of the training to deal with trauma, a team needs to have a frank discussion about what it will do in the case of a fallen or injured team member. In most specialized units, be they law enforcement or military, there is a common code that a team does not leave a fallen man behind. As a result, teams train on how to quickly and correctly perform buddy carries. An equally held concept of war is it is better to wound an adversary than kill them. This is because if a man is wounded, invariably his comrade in arms will come to his aid, hence, removing two fighters instead of one. On a protective operation, the ability to come to the aid of an injured or fallen comrade may not always be possible, or in the best interests of the mission.

If a protective detail is ever ambushed, the goal remains to move the protectee out of the kill zone and to a position of cover. If a team only consists of two members and one is injured, it will not be possible for the remaining member to come to the aid of his partner, while at the same time engage the adversary and deal with the protectee. The decision to leave a team member behind will no doubt be all the more difficult if the person is injured rather than dead. Obviously, if the team is larger, the ability for an immediate rescue is possible.

Every team needs to train in the methods of grabbing an injured team member and moving to a cover position, as well as into a vehicle for evacuation. At the same time, all team members need to realize that, under certain circumstances, any one of them may be left behind. They must not only defend themselves, but also provide for their own immediate medical attention. Perhaps the only consolation to this dilemma is that, unlike a military operation in some remote wilderness, in the modern urban setting an adversary is not likely to stay at the scene long, and once departed, the injured team member is much more likely to receive assistance from the local populace and/or responding police and medical personnel.

HAND-TO-HAND BASICS

It is amazing the number of people who do not know how to form a proper fist, let alone throw a punch. Perhaps, though, this is a good thing, given that a closed-fist punch to a head is more likely to break fingers than do much damage to the adversary. Keeping in mind that the main priority for a protective detail during an ambush is to break contact with an adversary and not necessarily take a person in custody or get into a drawn-out fight. Further, in an ambush situation, the adversary is either planning on killing or kidnapping the target; either way, they will need to deal with protective detail and, therefore, employ deadly force. Should a protective member get involved in a hand-to-hand combat situation with an adversary, they will need to counterattack quickly and violently and then leave. The focus, therefore, needs to be on the human body's weak points.

Fortunately, team members do not need to have earned their black belts in martial arts or train as cage fighters to be competent in hand-to-hand combat. A solid understanding of the body's vulnerable areas and the most effective methods of attack will enable team members to win. What follows is a partial list of those areas that can be attacked on an adversary's body, which will yield the greatest results:

Palm-heel strikes—As mentioned earlier, throwing closed-fist punches to an adversary's face is more likely to strike the hard skull bone, resulting in the breaking of one's fingers rather than causing damage to the adversary. Given that most people throw a punch with their dominate hand, breaking the fingers would prevent the use of one's firearm should the fight escalate to that level. For this reason, it is suggested that the palm strike be taught and practiced for attacks to the face. Thrown just as any other punch from the uppercut, hook, jab, and cross, the goal is to strike the opponent with the heel of the palm, that fleshy area right above the wrist (see Figure 4.6).

Pelvis strike—The region just under the navel encompassing the groin region, a strike to this area can have an almost instantaneous stunning effect on the adversary. It requires only approximately 400 pounds per square inch to rupture the pelvis.[21] This amount of force may sound impossible to generate, but is fairly easily achieved by a punch or a palm-heel strike (see Figure 4.7).

Ears strike—The human eardrum can rupture with only 6 pounds per square inch of pressure.[22] By striking both ears using cupped hands, a person can easily generate 12 pounds per square inch of pressure or more (see Figure 4.8). Having one's eardrums ruptured has an immediate stunning effect on the adversary and dramatically affects their equilibrium.

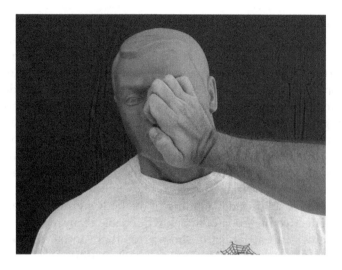

Figure 4.6 The palm-heel strike makes use of the fleshy part of the hand to deliver a blow while protecting the fingers.

Throat/trachea—Strikes or grabs to this region can have devastating effects that cause intense pain, all of which requires very little overall force to achieve. A word of caution: Strikes and grabs to this region can easily crush the trachea and lead to death and, therefore, should be considered deadly force. All practice should be conducted on a body opponent bag (see Figure 4.9).

Eye gouge—Only 52 pounds per square inch is required to rupture the human eye.[23] Merely touching someone's eyes causes immediate tearing and visual obstruction. Attacks to an adversary's eyes can be performed from a variety of positions including from behind (see Figure 4.10).

Elbows—They are a devastating weapon that even a small person can wield with great effect. Further, they are a body weapon that is very unlikely to be broken like fingers would be if made into a fist. The problem is they are often not taught, either for lack of knowledge or because they are deemed "too offensive" by departments. A close-in weapon, the goal is to strike an opponent with the area of the arm, just below the elbow (see Figure 4.11). It can be thrown from a number of angles, such as vertically, similar to a traditional upper cut to horizontally, which is similar to a hook punch, but all generally focused upon the adversary's face.

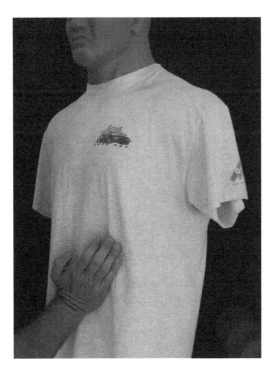

Figure 4.7 The pelvis strike is a powerful move, but it must be practiced to deliver correctly. Use of the bag with a shirt allows an individual to practice full power blows that are correctly targeted.

Head butt—Like elbows, it is another readily available, easy to use, devastating body weapon. Surprisingly, it is seldom taught to police recruits, which is unfortunate because it can be effective regardless of the size of the person employing it. Similarly, any attacker of any size, when struck in the face by another's cranium, is going to be at the very least momentarily stunned. The goal in using the head butt is to strike the adversary's face in the region of the eyes and nose with the crown of your head, the top of the forehead along the hairline (see Figure 4.12). You should stiffen your neck and keep your jaw closed when using this technique to prevent injuring yourself. One important note in targeting, you should avoid striking the adversary on his forehead, above the eyes, as this could cause you injury.

65

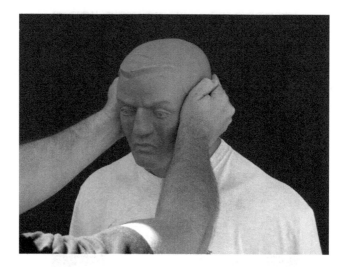

Figure 4.8 Use of the bag allows for correct targeting and the delivery of full power blows that would be impossible against a live training partner.

Figure 4.9 As with the blow to the ears, the bag allows for practice of strikes and grabs of the throat at full power.

Figure 4.10 Attacks to an adversary's eyes are easy to perform from a multitude of angles, all of which are immediately effective.

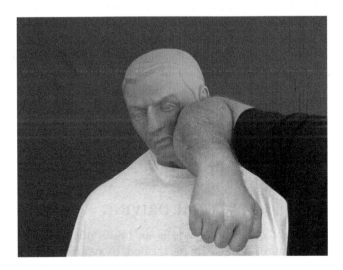

Figure 4.11 Practice delivering the elbow strike from a multitude of angles to best develop this potent close-quarters weapon.

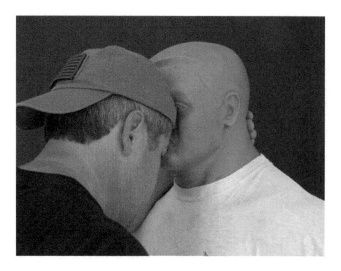

Figure 4.12 The head butt, like the elbow jam, is a powerful close-quarters weapon, but it must be practiced for correct targeting.

Sprawling and avoiding take-down—The ground is the last place any protective detail member wants to be in a fight. Even if you have the ground fighting skills of Royce Gracie, if you are on the ground because of being attacked, you are out of the game. The detail will be focused on protecting the principal and getting that person to a safe and fortified location and leaving you in the process. If you are charged by an adversary in a tackle-style attack, sprawl your legs back and wide, lowering your center of gravity, and preventing the take-down. If possible, force the adversary's head down to the ground using his momentum to help drive him into it. Depending on the nature of the attack, lethal blows could then be delivered.

TACTICAL DRIVING

Traveling in a protective motorcade is an important skill for teams to acquire. While it may seem easily performed, there are nuances that will separate the professional from the amateur. The basic concept of driving in a motorcade is relatively straight forward. Obtaining direct training is always preferred, but, given the level of driver training most law enforcement officers have received, coupled with their experience, just learning the basic concepts of a motorcade may suffice (refer to Dale June's book *Introduction to Executive Protection* (CRC Press, 1999) for an excellent set of drawings detailing motorcade operations). From this point, it just requires practice to dial it in.

When traveling in a multivehicle motorcade, communication between drivers is critical, especially when moving at a high rate of speed. Much of this communication can be nonverbal, if the drivers have trained with each other. When two or more vehicles are traveling in a motorcade, the goal will be to limit the distance between them to around five feet in order to prevent any other vehicle on the road from pulling in between them.

For the second or third vehicle driving behind the first on a highway at between 55 and 75 mph, such a close distance can be unnerving. If all vehicles have dark-tinted windows, the second and third vehicles view of the road can be greatly reduced. For this reason, the first car should drive on the right side of a lane, allowing for the second vehicle to be on the left side and thus having a view of the road ahead. However, for a third vehicle, this may not work as well. If a team deployed a third vehicle and had access to a sufficiently powerful sport utility vehicle (SUV), it could be positioned here, providing an overview of the road ahead.

While every member of the team should be thoroughly briefed on the routes to be traveled to limit the amount of communication between cars, there will still be a need to talk to one another. Lane changes are one of the most common needs. It is the front or lead vehicle that makes the determination of a lane change and signals with their vehicle turn signals (or by direct radio/cell phone communication). The lane change, however, begins with the last vehicle in the motorcade to local down the desired lane, allowing for the first and second vehicles to follow suit.

Evasive, high-performance driving requires practical and professional training at specialized facilities. It is at these locations where team members can learn such techniques as forward and reverse 180° turns. Once team members have learned the mechanics of these turns and are competent on an individual level, they must practice them as a team, that is, a motorcade of two and three vehicles employing reverse 180°s at the same time. It is only then that a team will be completely trained and comfortable in their use. Of note: Just as shooting skills require maintenance to prevent deterioration, the same applies to driving skills.

Beyond specialized driving techniques, another equally important aspect of evasive high-speed driving is the effective use of the entire width of a lane, positioning on entering and exiting corners, and steering and braking control. As Isaac Newton stated in his first law, "an object in motion tends to stay in motion." Hence, a vehicle's momentum wants to continue in the direction it is traveling. When a driver wants to turn, he is going against the direction of the vehicle's momentum. If the driver does not slow the speed or momentum of the vehicle sufficiently and/or turns too sharply, the vehicle's momentum will overwhelm the suspension and traction resulting in a loss of control. By taking the straightest line through a curve or turn with the correct amount of brake and accelerator, the driver is able to use the vehicle's momentum to maximum benefit.

During any escape from a threat, whether on foot or in a vehicle, the goal is to avoid moving in a straight line and/or in a predictable manner. As every new army recruit learns in boot camp, when rushing from one location to another, the key is to run in a zigzag fashion to prevent an enemy from obtaining an easy target. The same holds true when in a vehicle. When fleeing an ambush, drivers will want to break out of the line of sight of the ambush location as soon as possible. This requires making a turn at the earliest opportunity. Going into a high-speed turn incorrectly can easily result in the vehicle losing its priceless traction and the driver, control of the vehicle. If a crash occurs within close proximity to the location, the adversary could be provided with another opportunity to accomplish the objective.

The goal for the driver is to keep the vehicle moving as fast as possible through the corner. This requires applying the correct amount of brake going into it and the right amount of accelerator coming out. Unlike a professional race car, the vehicles that law enforcement officers drive do not have top-of-the-line suspension and tires, which all have a great affect on vehicle control in a turn.

This then requires the driver to develop his or her feel for the vehicle. As one driving instructor once told the author, "It is driving by the seat of your pants." This is a very appropriate statement as good drivers will be able to feel the vehicle and know when they are close to losing control. What the driver is "feeling" for is the vehicle's weight transfer coupled with the feel of the steering wheel and tire traction. Every corner is made up of three parts, the entry, the apex, and the exit. The driver who can travel the straightest line through the corner will generally be able to maintain the greatest amount of speed through it. While it may seem cool and fast to take a vehicle through a corner as though it was "on rails," this is rarely quicker. In fact, professional road racers, from GT sport cars to Formula 1, always follow a line through a corner that has the straightest path.

As the vehicle approaches the point of the "turn in" toward the corner, it is the point where the vehicle is most sensitive to weight transfer. As the corner approaches, the driver should position the vehicle for a high entry. Therefore, to make a right turn, the driver positions the vehicle on the extreme left side of the lane. As the entry approaches, the driver applies the brake in steady hard fashion or full force limit. This threshold braking allows the driver to slow the vehicle to the desired speed as quickly as possible, while the vehicle is still traveling in a straight line. The threshold braking ends as the vehicle reaches the turn-in point. The vehicle will still be moving at a considerable rate as the driver turns the vehicle. While adding throttle to maintain the speed, the driver reaches the "apex" or inside of the corner, which in this example is on the far right side of the lane. As the vehicle reaches the apex of the corner, the driver begins to apply more speed, taking the vehicle straight to the far left side of the lane. As the exit point is reached, the driver applies full throttle.

Ultimately, the more turns motorcade vehicles can rapidly put between them and their adversary, the more likely they will successfully escape. This requires team members to practice the technique whenever the opportunity presents itself. If a driver regularly practices using the full width of a lane during normal driving, then, when the worst case happens, the driver will have already developed the habit. Some long curvy roads and some portions of highways allow for good practice at speed (obviously, for legal and safety reasons, one does not want to push the vehicle to the point of the extreme on public roads). Should there be portions of roadway that, due to the environment, are regularly traveled, agencies may want to consider closing them down during periods of low use. This would allow the drivers to conduct test runs, providing them the opportunity to determine exactly how fast they can take a turn. That knowledge could make all the difference one day.

Another part of evasive driving that some schools teach is the use of ramming as a method of escaping a blockade, consisting of a vehicle or two positioned across the roadway. While these techniques are quite effective, the modern safety features of automobiles have largely removed this from a driver's repertoire. Unless a vehicle has installed airbag kill switches as discussed in Chapter 2, ramming another vehicle is no longer an option. Beyond the effects on a driver of being struck by an airbag moving at approximately 200 mph, some vehicles engines will shut down upon airbag deployment. The increasing use of side-impact airbags on vehicles also could cause issues should a driver attempt a PIT or reverse PIT maneuver if not positioned correctly.

Ramming a vehicle by rapidly reversing directly into the adversary also can be problematic, given modern safety features. In some vehicles, an impact on the rear end of a vehicle will cause an automatic shutdown of the fuel line (this can occur if a vehicle spins beyond a certain degree, such as what happens when performing certain evasive maneuvers). Considering the history of attacks on motorcades, these safety features could, in fact, jeopardize lives. Given the nature of government fleet services and the issues of liability, circumventions of these safety features are likely to be hard-fought battles with the bureaucrats. If unable to install kill switches, it is critical that drivers understand how their vehicle will respond to certain techniques (when in doubt, see the local dealer mechanics for more information).

The difference in power-to-weight ratios of most vehicles on the road today is confined to a relatively narrow range. These ranges are further restricted, depending on personnel and equipment, that is, the "payload weight" in a vehicle. Modern vehicles have reached the point as well where accelerating from a stop to 60 miles per hour ranges from 3.8 to 10.3 seconds, be it a turbo Porsche or a Toyota Corolla. Therefore, trying to outrun a vehicle along a straight run, lacking a considerable head start, is almost pointless. This is especially true in that the adversary will better be able to place shots on target if your escape route is straight. It is in situations such as these, camber bars shine (see Chapter 3 for more detailed information).

One form of training that can be easily overlooked and/or not practiced, given the inherent difficulties, is dealing with the disabling of a security driver during a motorcade. One of the most effective ways of stopping a motorcade is to disable the security driver operating the vehicle, and this has been used in many targeted attacks around the world. Kill or severely injure the driver, and the more likely it is that the vehicle will come to a stop. As with some of the evasive maneuvers, this skill needs to be learned from professionals and practiced at a location designed for specialized driving.

Part of the knowledge cycle for any type of tactical unit is understanding your own weakness. Sun Tzu's advice on knowing yourself can and should be expanded to include your equipment. What are the limitations of your weapons in terms of effective range and ballistic effects? What are the limitations of your vehicles and what do they impose on a protective team? For instance, the Ford Taurus, which is often purchased by government fleet services, has rear passenger windows that are fairly small. Even if the rear window completely opened, it would be extremely difficult for an operator to field a subgun or rifle effectively from such a portal.

Remember that every tactic and technique offers a certain amount of inherent strengths and weaknesses. These need to be thoroughly thought out and understood by the team prior to their employment. Once in an ambush situation, you are in the worst-case scenario, and it is too late to identify a problem. Only by developing and training repeatedly in immediate action drills with your teammates and equipment, will you have a chance beyond just plain luck.

PRACTICAL EXERCISES

The gold standard in tactical training, force-on-force exercises provides a team with the opportunity to apply all of its skills and experience to a scenario. It allows the team members the opportunity to elevate their heart rates to the point of experiencing the loss of motor skills. It also allows team leaders as well as the individual team members to identify mistakes made, tactics that work or do not work, standard operating procedures that need to be modified or developed, etc. While role players unknown to the team are ideal in scenario-based training, even splitting a team into two groups, one playing the part of the adversary and the other the part of the protective unit provides beneficial results.

An additional outcome of having team members play the role of adversaries, they begin to develop their own strategies on carrying out an attack on a targeted individual. This can be extremely beneficial to the team later as they begin conducting advance site surveys and route analysis for future protective operations. These exercises should cover all aspects of the job, including formations while moving on foot with various numbers of protective members, motorcade movements (again with varying numbers of vehicles), and, of course, immediate action drills to ambushes.

To achieve the most benefits from scenario-based training, especially in developing the automatic response to ambush attacks, requires the use of weapons. The recent development of Airsoft weapons has provided teams that ability to train using the same weapons they carry on protective operations, all at a significant savings over some of the other paint-/soap-based systems (see Figure 4.13). The similarities between Airsoft weapons and their real counterparts are extraordinary, allowing for the continued used of muscle memory in deploying them.

Flashbangs are an excellent tool for use in training a team to respond to IED-based attacks. Thankfully, here in North America, explosive-based

Figure 4.13 The similarities between the Colt 1911 and the Airsoft version of 1911 allow for effective training with the same weapon system characteristics.

attacks are relatively rare. That is not to say, however, that they have not been known to occur. It is, therefore, incumbent for every team to spend some time training to deal with these types of attacks. It is here that flashbangs, especially those with replaceable inserts, are an extremely effective tool.

While nowhere near a real explosive blast and lacking access to a military ground burst simulator, a flashbang provides an excellent way for a team to develop their reaction to a blast. Granted, there is no accompanying fragmentation or shrapnel, but there is a concussion, noise, and blinding flash. If nothing else, it allows the team to learn to respond, to know, and function as though they are under attack. It is effective in simulating an IED detonation that has perhaps disabled a vehicle. Practice vehicle deboarding, regrouping in remaining vehicles, and exit. Adding a smoke canister can greatly increase the "confusion" potential a team would have to work through.

TRAINING TO CONDUCT AN ATTACK

As part of a protective unit's training to respond and counter their adversary, it will benefit a team, including analysts, to develop a deep understanding of a "hit." While this may be a somewhat controversial topic, the more a protective operator and/or analyst understands the dynamics involved in planning and carrying out a targeted attack, the better they will be able to perceive potential ambush sites. Fortunately, much of this can occur on a law enforcement range, and should start at the most basic level. Begin with the practice inside of the distances of 25 feet (eventually to be brought down to the extreme close range). Armed with an Airsoft or Simunition weapon, have each operator and analyst practice taking out a human target within these distances? On the defensive/protective side of the practice, the team gains the benefit of training for possible attacks. As most teams do not move around with their weapons drawn, while the suspects *will*, the practice/training needs to proceed this way.

Ideally, this would then be improved upon by using the same training methods but taken to locations such as vacant homes and military MOUT (military operations in urban terrain) sites. In locations such as these, the "assassins" and the team would really be able to explore the strengths and weaknesses with their plans, methods, and tactics to deal with an attack. Those individuals playing the role of the attacker would gain the necessary insight into what is needed to carry out such an attack.

My last thoughts on training of protective teams are the need to practice in the types of environments in which you could end up operating. This means conducting training at times of reduced light and even nighttime hours. This means conducting training in the rain and snow. Teams need to know how to deal with protective operations while wearing more bulky clothing, perhaps an umbrella, etc. Some of it can be uncomfortable, but it needs to happen (some of my fondest memories are while training or operating in bad weather, miserable to the core but working as a team). Although, to be fair, the training or operational experience was always more enjoyable in hindsight—and after having a hot shower and a cold beer.

ENDNOTES

1. *Sharpening the Warrior's Edge: The Psychology and Science of Training*, by Bruce K. Siddle, PPCT Research Publications, October 1995, 148.

2. *Psychological Effects of Combat* by Dave Grossman and Bruce K. Siddle, Academic Press, 2000, www.killology.com.

3. Ibid.

4. Bumgarner, Jeffrey, William J. Lewinski, William Hudson, and Sgt. Craig Sapp. An Examination of Police Officer Chronometry: I Swear … I Don't Know How I Shot Him in the Back, *The Scene: The Journal of The Association for Crime Scene Reconstruction.*

5. Ibid.

6. Ibid.

7. Gunmen Ambush Security Official's Convoy in Mexico, *BBC News*, April 25, 2010, http://news.bbc.co.uk/2/hi/8642452.stm.

8. *Targeted Violence: A Statistical and Tactical Analysis of Assassinations, Contract Killings and Kidnappings,* by Glenn P. McGovern. CRC Press, Boca Raton, FL., 2010.

9. Ibid., p. 138.

10. Ibid., p. 82, 105.

11. Targeted by drug cartels, Mexican politician quickly relocates by Kevin G. Hall, McClatchy newspapers, August 10, 2008, http://www.dallasnews.com/sharedcontent/dws/news/world/mexico/stories/DN-mexico_10int.ART.State.Edition1.4dabac1.html.

12. Central Bank Deputy Chairman Andrey Kozlov Murdered, *Komersant*, September 15, 2006, http://www.kommersant.com/p705012/Central_Bank_ Deputy_Chairman_Andrey_Kozlov_Murdered.

13. Fortuyn Suspect Admits Murder, *BBC News*, Thursday, March 27, 2003, http://news.bbc.co.uk/2/hi/europe/2888859.stm, (accessed March 28, 2003).

14. Medgar Evers, http://naacp.com/about/history/megarevers/index.htm.

15. McGovern, *Targeted Violence,* coupled with ongoing research into organized targeted attacks.

16. Top Anti-Terror Chief Dies in Spain Bombing, *Sky News*, June 19, 2009, http://news.sky.com/skynews/Home/World-News/Car-Bomb-Top-Anti-Terror-Chief-Killed-In-Spanish-City-Bilbao-In-Basque-Country/Article/200 906315312184?lid=ARTICLE_15312184_CarBomb:TopAntiTerrorChiefKilled InSpanishCityBilbaoInBasqueCountry&lpos=searchresults.

17. McGovern, *Targeted Violence*, p. 120.

18. *The Operators: On the Streets with 14 Company—The Army's Top Secret Elite,* by James Rennie, Century, London, 1996, 234 pages.

19. Guatemala Zeta Camp Raid, STRATFOR Mexico Security Memo: March 30, 2009, http://www.stratfor.com/analysis/20090330_mexico_security_memo_march_30_2009.

20. McGovern, *Targeted Violence*, p. 89.

21. Ibid.

22. Ibid.

23. Ibid.

5

Assessing the Risk and Threat of Hostile Organizations

Those who cannot remember the past are condemned to repeat it.

George Santayana
Philosopher (1905)

On the evening of Tuesday, June 16, 2009, James Amburn, an American banker and financial advisor, was kidnapped from his home in Speyer, Germany. The adversaries in this case can perhaps only be described as history's most usual crew of kidnappers to ever target another individual. Amburn arrived at his residence to find four men, all retirees with an age range of between 57 and 80 years of age. They had traveled from their homes in Bavaria, a distance of some 280 miles. Amburn had been the advisor for these men and when the economy turned downward, they lost approximately $5 million in investments in the U.S. real estate market.

During the discussion that followed their arrival at Amburn's home, one of the men mentioned to another to get the green folder from the car. Unbeknownst to Amburn, this was the signal to start the kidnap. Amburn was quickly overpowered and disabled by having his hands, knees, and feet bound with duct tape. He was then put into a wooden box that the men had previous constructed. The box with Amburn inside was placed into the trunk of the kidnappers' Audi 8 sedan and driven back to one of the men's homes near the Austrian border. Amburn was held prisoner for four days in a basement cell until his rescue by law enforcement. All four elderly men, along with their elderly wives, were arrested and ultimately convicted of the crime.[1]

This amazing story provides definitive proof that one can never know with any certainty when or if he or she may be a target for organized violence. This extends to law enforcement and security agencies, where determining the presence and level of risk an individual may face can be difficult to assess, even when the potential threat source and target are known. When neither is known, conducting assessments requires a different set of analytical processes, a little skill, resources, and even luck. In the years following the September 11 attacks in New York City and Washington, D.C., much has been said about "connecting the dots" by government intelligence agencies, and how there were failures and missed opportunities. Conducting a threat assessment against an adversary can be extremely difficult, let alone against an unknown hostile group. Rather than connecting the dots, it is more akin to putting together a jigsaw puzzle without having all the pieces, not knowing if you can find all the pieces, or how many pieces there are in the first place, and finally having no idea what the finished picture looks like.

Much of the current literature dealing with threat assessments is from the perspective that the "threatening" party is known to the victim and/ or authorities (including corporate security). These cases typically fall into categories of stalking, mental illness, domestic violence, and antisocial subjects. However, in examining organized targeted killings and kidnappings perpetrated against government representatives and corporate executives over the past 60 years, many were attacked without ever receiving a threat. Alternatively, if threats were received, the individuals issuing the threat never identified themselves and, more importantly, the hostile parties tasked with conducting the attack were not known or believed to have a direct link to the victim.

Organized targeted attacks are by their nature difficult to foresee. The individuals in control of these groups are often dedicated and secretive. This makes confirming the threat they represent and, more importantly, preempting them exceedingly difficult. The type of organization the threat stems from also presents assessment problems. Terrorist organizations tend to have a longer time horizon in which to strike. Further, should a particular target be deemed too difficult to reach, they can easily switch to another and still accomplish their political goal.

Conversely, criminal groups tend to have a much more constricted time frame in which to strike. They also tend to focus on a specific individual causing them problems. However, if the target is determined to be too difficult to reach, the organization may decide to cancel the hit. Whatever the situation, the calculus is murky as law enforcement and/ or security will most likely never know with certainty if the threat has expired or is still viable. Explaining to management why an increased level of security is needed to protect against an undefined threat is a challenge, especially when scarce resources need to be applied elsewhere. Caution must be used as uncertainty can be made into a rationale to wait until more information is developed. Sometimes this is the correct step to take, but is a team or department willing to take the chance? Therefore, it must be communicated that protective units cannot guarantee complete security and, more importantly, individuals must understand they bear significant responsibility for their own security.

A potential mitigator to this problem is through the employment of a Design-Basis Risk Management/Assessment Model. This model allows an individual or organization to determine the assets most likely to be targeted for violence, the current threat picture, and vulnerabilities that an adversary could exploit to accomplish his goal. The mission of the Design-Basis Risk Management/Assessment Model is to determine the potential for a specific and limited number of unwanted events to occur, such as a targeted killing or kidnapping, and to develop an appropriate response in advance. The assessment involves analyzing three factors:

1. *Asset identification*—Anything of value to an organization including and, most important, personnel.
2. *Vulnerability assessment*—Any weakness that an adversary could exploit.
3. *Threat assessment*—The capability and intention of an adversary to carry out a targeted attack.

Asset identification is the first stage and perhaps most important in conducting a risk assessment. The focus is placed on those resources that are the most critical to the organization, which for this work means personnel. While all staff members are important, it is impossible to assess and/or provide security for everyone. Hence, the focus needs to be on the key individuals of the organization, usually the leadership. The nature of the organization will dictate who else should be focused on. Using a prosecutorial office as an example, the asset focus could be initially on those individuals most likely to be targeted. Prosecutors assigned to gang, organized crime, corruption, and drug cases would have the priority.

Vulnerability assessment seeks to identify exploitable situations that an adversary could use to target his victim. This could stem from a general lack of security and/or personal behavior. As with the threat assessment, the analysis is performed from the perspective of the adversaries. How would they look at the asset/target? Is there enough perceivable vulnerability to allow them to carry out a hit? For some hostile organizations, if asset vulnerability is low, resulting in a "hard target," they may decide to employ a different technique in order to accomplish their goal. Hence, the critical need to examine the assets from the perspective of each adversary known to be present in your area or jurisdiction. Hostile groups do not often operate in the same fashion, for example, in the San Francisco Bay area, there are a number of Latino gangs, as well as several outlaw motorcycle groups (OMGs), and environmental and racial extremists, among others. Each has a different attack history to include weapons of choice (i.e., handguns versus explosives) and tactics. For each group, ask:

1. How would I (a member of whatever group) target this individual?
2. Is the target a creature of habit, providing more opportunities to strike?
3. How much cyber information is available?

The cyber threat to assets is an important aspect of the vulnerability assessment. While generally considered an issue traditionally faced by computer networks, the amount of cyber-based information available to a hostile organization regarding its target must be identified. The primary reason is that the greater amount of cyber information there is available, the easier it becomes for the adversary to develop his attack plans and strategies without ever leaving the security of his base of operations. This, therefore, decreases his own vulnerability to early compromise and detection by authorities. Additionally, the presence of a cyber photograph of a target is exceedingly helpful to a hostile group.

The use of photographs to assist those tasked by an organization to properly identify its target is well documented—from Nazi SS hitmen killing individuals, leading up to and during World War II, to contract killers hired by gangs, organized crime families, and even corporate rivals. All have used photos of their intended victims. When a recent quality photograph that also confirms the identity of the target is available online, the hostile group has been given a huge advantage.

One of the greatest advantages a hostile organization has when targeting an individual is anonymity. When the assassins are not known or linked to a target or the target's organization, while at the same time are able to identify their victim, they can close within striking distance with significantly reduced chances of detection.

When conducting the assessment of vulnerability, most of the information should be obtained by interviewing the asset (targeted individual). Equally important is the interview of the family of the target in order to obtain their perspectives. It should also include some form of physical surveillance and reconnaissance of the asset to identify those vulnerability factors of the daily routine that the person is either unaware of or does not want to admit to. Others may minimize the threat or are in denial, which in turn can lead to less accurate details being provided. The physical checks assist in taking some of the guess work out and help to ensure that the analyst is, in fact, looking from the outside in.

Threat assessment is the next stage in the analysis and focuses on the potential adversaries that could target the asset. In any threat assessment, it is vital that intuition and assumption be replaced "with a reliance on data and information obtained from research and interviews."[2] It must be conducted from the perspective of the adversary, not the individual conducting the analysis. Adversaries, obviously, include those individuals and organizations known to be operating in your area. Gangs, organized crime groups, drug trafficking organizations, and terrorist groups are, of course, a rich source of potential threats.

Therefore, in order to narrow the focus, begin at least initially with those groups/assailants that have the proven *intent* and *capability* to conduct a targeted attack. This should then be coupled with their *history* of conducting such operations. Obtaining this information will most likely require the use of outside expert assistance (ideally at the more localized level). Using a violent street gang as an example to determine the intent and capability, these are some of the questions that need to be answered:

1. What are the membership numbers of the gang?
2. How many are capable, or who would most likely be tasked, to plan and/or carry out the attack?
3. Which of those individuals are not currently in custody (and what is their background)?
4. Who in the organization has the authority to order the attack, and what is his background and current location (i.e., jail, on the street, etc.)?
5. What types of weaponry are they known or believed to have access to?
6. Are any members known to have a military background?

7. Are they known or suspected of training for operations?
8. Is there any history of targeted attacks (keeping in mind that targeting one of the organization's own members or even a rival gang member is far different from targeting a judge, a prosecutor, or similar figure)? Even if there is no history of attacks, does the criminal organization encourage or allow attacks on law enforcement, etc.?
9. Is there any current reason that is likely to increase the possibility of conducting a targeted attack (such as an ongoing criminal case against a leader of the gang)?
10. Are they linked to more sophisticated groups, indicating a possible exchange or proliferation of expertise and/or weaponry?
11. Would the hostile organization consider outsourcing a hit? (While rare, there is precedent.)

Risk assessment: How likely is it that an adversary or adversaries can and will attack those identified? Some, perhaps *most*, of this will depend upon the hostile organization's history. What are the most likely vulnerabilities that the adversary may decide to exploit against the identified assets? Many risk models incorporate a number system of between 1–5 or 1–10. The goal is to assist the analyst, not only in determining the level of risk but also to be in a position to articulate the threat to management (Figure 5.1).

Once the amount of risk a specific person or organization represents is determined, countermeasures can be developed. The process of risk assessment is an ongoing methodology. New threats will emerge as old ones fade. A process of continuous assessment allows for the monitoring of risks and helps to address them in the most effective and timely manner.

ASSESSING A HOSTILE ORGANIZATION

Conducting a threat assessment of a hostile organization is very different from those conducted on a single identified individual. When an individual makes a threat against another, a complete background is conducted. The person's criminal, civil, and psychological history is reviewed and analyzed extensively. The hostile individual's support network can be brought into the fold to assist in alleviating, mitigating, and managing the threat. Conversely, when the threat stems from a hostile organization, the threat assessment becomes more complicated. This is primarily because

	Threat Factors				Threat Level (1–8)	Method of Attack A, firearms; B, sniper; C, explosives
Threat	Existence (1)	Violent History (1)	Intentions (2)	Targeting (4)		
1						
2						
3						
4						
5						
6						
7						
8						
9						
10						

Figure 5.1 The Risk Model Sheet sample gives the analyst the ability to gauge the level of a threat.

identifying who in the organization will be tasked with carrying out the attack often is not possible. However, in some ways, it can be easier than the lone individual.

A command structure of a criminal or terrorist organization will often be a bit more rational than that of the single individual when ordering a targeted attack. The hostile organization realizes to some degree the potential adverse effects stemming from the killing of a government official. They will have performed in some manner a cost-benefit analysis of the targeted killing. Will the government response outweigh the threat the targeted individual represents to the organization? If not, then the hit may proceed as planned. While this is most applicable to criminal organizations that are economically driven rather than ideologically as with terrorist organizations, it does not mean it is not taken into consideration. Many terrorist organizations count on the support of the local populace. If through a killing the terrorist/extremists lose support, the economic loss could affect their ability to carry out future operations.

Case in point: Before dawn on Thursday, August 26, 2010, in Reggio Calabria, Italy, the home of Magistrate Salvatore Di Landro was hit by the blast of an improvised explosive device. The force of the blast shattered windows and ripped open the steel-barred security door, but did not injure the magistrate or his wife, both of whom were home at the time. The magistrate was assigned to antimafia prosecutions at the time of the attack.

This attack had been preceded on January 3, 2010, by a middle-of-the-night bombing of the main courthouse in Reggio. This was followed shortly afterward with a single bullet mailed to another magistrate assigned to antimafia crimes. In late January, an improvised explosive device cached inside of a vehicle was discovered positioned along the route to be traveled by the motorcade of Italian President Giorgio Napolitano. In June, Magistrate Di Landro was told by his mechanics that the lug nuts of all four wheels of his car had been significantly loosened. Perhaps most significantly, in July 2010, some 300 'Ndrangheta mafia suspects had been arrested by the Italian authorities.[3]

The preceding case is a perfect example of the cost-benefit analysis process in effect. With the 'Ndrangheta leadership suffering from several hundred members in custody and facing serious time behind bars, they would appear to have few options remaining. If they cannot successfully intimidate the Italian judicial system, their organization will probably be severely crippled. What is interesting are the incremental steps that transpired in their effort to obtain their goal of intimidation without the costly effect that comes with the targeted killing of a magistrate. As of this writing, the 'Ndrangheta have not conducted a targeted attack against a government official. Even in this case, while conceivable, it is difficult to know with any certainty if they will take that final step.

This process of taking the path of least resistance in obtaining their goal against a government official is not uncommon. It has been documented from as far back as Al Capone's crew, to the Sicilian mafia during the 1980s, through to the modern Mexican drug cartels. When dealing with a government official, whether a local cop or a sitting senator, the criminal group may initially try to corrupt that person, to pay-off that individual who has become a problem for that hostile organization prior to conducting a hostile act.[4]

When, or if, this does not work, the adversary often begins threats and intimidation. This can take the form of phone calls, threatening letters, photos mailed of family members, and menacing strangers loitering near the target's home, office, or frequented location(s). The adversary may

make attempts to accomplish the goals against their target using other corrupt officials. If all of this fails, then the adversary may come to the conclusion that a more extreme next step is necessary and attempt to kill the target or a family member.

> *Case in point*: In 2006, David Figueroa was the mayor of Agua Prieta, a town in the Mexican state of Sonoma and, more importantly, a key location on the route of drug traffic into the United States. The cartels attempted to corrupt Figueroa, but he refused. Not long afterward, his father was attacked, but luckily survived.[5]

A similar methodology may be employed to dissuade witnesses from testifying, or the decision is made that the individual needs to be killed. This can be especially true if the witness is one of the organization's own members. Regardless, those tasked with providing protection should have knowledge of the threats received by their protectee (given that individual has actually advised someone) and the group responsible.

> *Case in point*: In 2009, a witness to a homicide in San Francisco was murdered at his home approximately 60 miles away in another town and county. What is interesting regarding this attack was that the victim's office/business was in a more seedy part of town and the murder, which he had witnessed, occurred on the street in front of the business. It would seem that the victim was in the most danger in the evening hours at the business location and not in front of his home.[6]

If, however, the adversary is targeting the individual out of revenge for some real or perceived wrong, then there is a strong likelihood that without inside informant information, advance knowledge of the danger will not be known.

> *Case in point*: In January 2001, information was received by law enforcement that two prosecutors in Santa Clara County, a husband and wife team, had been "green lighted," meaning an order had come down by the then command of a notorious and dangerous California Mexican prison gang, for both to be killed. This targeted attack was ordered because, a few years prior, the prosecutors had successfully prosecuted a former "general" of the prison gang as part of a large-scale, multiagency task force investigating the hostile organization. The hit was to be a "gift" to that gang leader. It was also learned that at least one gang member had boasted of following the couple to the courthouse.[7]

Whatever the circumstances, when the exact nature, source, or even presence of a threat is unknown, the threat analyst must employ different tools. The types of these assessment tools are more closely aligned with that found in counterterrorism investigations. When you consider the nature of targeted attacks, assassination, and kidnapping, along with the FBI's definition of terrorism—"the unlawful use of *force* or *violence* against persons or property to *intimidate* or *coerce* a government, the *civilian* population, or any segment thereof, in furtherance of political or social objectives"—it becomes clearer that this approach is appropriate.

In those instances where the hostile group/organization is known, an assessment on the group itself must first be performed. Understanding the threat potential of any group requires first, information about the behavior relevant to the suspected event, in this case a targeted attack. What events have or will be taking place that could cause the hostile organization to consider such an attack? Once the analyst determines the group's willingness to conduct a targeted attack, an assessment of those members most likely to be tasked and/or willing and able to see it through should follow.

In order to understand the threat a potential hostile group represents, it is necessary to understand the four key principles of group behavior.[8]

1. What are the organizations attitudes and opinions?
2. What process does the organization follow in decision making?
3. What are the motivating factors of the group?
4. What are the group's norms (including a history of responses)?

When evaluating a group's decision-making process, keep in mind that certain decisions may follow a different process. For example, with the Sicilian mafia during the 1980s, the decision to target a government official required an agreement of the entire council (made up of representatives of each major family), rather than that of just one or more families. It is conceivable that, with most hostile organizations, the decision to conduct an attack against a witness or informant could probably be made at a "local" level. The decision to target a government official would most logically be one made at the highest levels. Given the amount of expected blowback in carrying out such an attack, the decision would not be reached quickly. However, as has been seen in attacks by groups, such as the Sicilian mafia, drug cartels, and even prison gangs, it is entirely possible for a rogue cell to go out on its own—then all bets are off.

Determining a group's motivation for carrying out a targeted attack is perhaps the most important element in obtaining understanding. What level of threat/risk would members of an organization (court staff, prosecutorial office, city and/or county government seat, etc.) be facing? Would such an event generate the media notoriety for the group that is commonly sought after by terror groups? Would such an attack possibly reduce a government's willingness to pursue the group, a motivator also with terror organizations, but perhaps more commonly associated with criminal organizations? Part of this would be the group's cohesiveness. Is there an internal power struggle in which a targeted attack could focus a government response on a rival faction to the benefit of the other? Understanding the threat potential of any group requires information about the behavior relevant to the suspected event, in this case a killing.

A key component in understanding an organization's norms requires identification of the rules or standards under which an organization functions. This requires knowledge of the organization's structure, the group cohesiveness, and their current situation.[9] The level of the organization's cohesiveness would indicate the level of control by the upper echelons. It could also indicate the potential for rogue behavior. To this, consideration is given to the group's history or past practice in similar situations. Knowledge of these points could/would lead to more detailed information of who would make and/or be involved in the decision to target a government official.

The group's current situation also can provide insight into its decision-making processes. Is the group at war with a rival? Are key members lost, either deceased or in jail. Is the internal structure in disarray? Disarray at the organizational level sometimes leads to more difficult assessments as there is more potential for unpredictable attacks from a "lone wolf" member of the organization. These factors could indicate a decrease in risk, given a hostile organization's need to "lay low" and/or prevent it from being heavily targeted by authorities. However, it is critical to remember that individuals belonging to criminal and extremist groups, even different cultures, do not necessarily think or see things logically or the way others in society would.

Identifying who would be tasked with carrying out the job and what form it most likely would take would be the next stages of the analysis. Historically, how has the organization perpetrated similar attacks? If they have never targeted a government official in the past, how did they carry out other attacks on lesser targets? Remember that groups and individuals tend to stick with what they know and with what has worked for them. More than likely, the organization will follow a similar path to their objective, be it a rival or a government official.

Determining who will most likely be tasked to carry out such an operation requires more detailed knowledge of the organization's membership and leadership. In the Sicilian mafia during the 1980s, it was a matter of honor to carry out a high-profile attack. As a result, it would be given to an individual farther up the organizational ladder. Regardless, the attack would have to be performed by someone in the area capable of handling the job. That would mean the subject was in the country, state, or county and not in jail. That person or those persons would have to have the resolve, the intelligence, and the ability to carry it out.

Just as in any legitimate organization, not everyone will have the same skills set. Therefore, when conducting a risk assessment upon any hostile organization, it is important that the individuals with the detailed knowledge of the group be contacted; this may include former members or those disenfranchised with the group. These experts will be able to identify those out on the street (i.e., not in jail or deceased) that would have the skills and mentality to carry out a targeted attack. This obviously would allow for a more focused analysis and can lead to a significant reduction in the number of individuals investigators would have to background and assess.

When analyzing specific individuals within an organization that could be tasked with carrying out a targeted attack, consider the following factors:

1. *Desire*—Is the individual a dedicated member of the organization looking to make a name for himself? Does he have a level of commitment that would drive him to carry out the operation regardless of the potential outcomes (i.e., death or prison)?
2. *Ability*—Beyond the resources of a hostile organization, does the individual have the skill set necessary to plan, organize, and carry out a targeted attack? Obtaining the individual's arrest and if applicable, military records will provide some the answers to *desire* and *ability.*

While there have been documented incidents of hostile organizations outsourcing a targeted attack, these have fortunately been few and far between. If a group has been known to outsource any of its criminal activities, then this possibility should be factored into the total risk assessment. The difficulty with assessing such risk is that the "contractor" will not necessarily conform to the norms, structure, etc., of the ordering organization. Once the assignment has been given to the contractor, that individual can carry it out, however and whenever they see fit (depending on the agreed parameters). This is then one of the primary reasons for having knowledge of the attack cycle covered later in this chapter.

> *Case in point:* On September 14, 1987, a Monday night in Biloxi, Mississippi, Judge Vincent Sherry, Jr. and his wife Margaret were assassinated inside of their home by a lone assassin who used a suppressed .22 caliber pistol. In the subsequent investigation, it was learned the assassin lived in Texas and had been hired by members of the Dixie Mafia to kill the judge, apparently over an issue involving money. The killer had traveled from his home state two days before the attack and found the residence. He then returned later on the night of the 14th and was able to surreptitiously enter the house before killing the couple.[10]

THE "WHAT IF" ANALYSIS

Once the known groups in your area of operations have been assessed, the next stage is to conduct a "what if" analysis. This technique begins by assuming that an attack has already occurred. It is sort of a "reverse engineering" of the event. Its focus is not on the significance of the attack, or the ultimate consequences, but rather on how it might be perpetrated. The purpose is to initially remove the judgment on the likelihood of a targeted attack occurring to allow a more focused analysis of the events that would lead up to such an event. Perhaps one of the best attributes of this analysis is that it can be conducted using *limited information*.

The first step in this methodology is to define the hostile event. For example, let us say that the event was an attempted shooting of a prosecutor by members of a prison gang that occurs at the residence (which is statistically the location with the highest probability of such an event).[11] The analyst would map out the process that would need to be followed in order for such an event to occur, to reverse-engineer the attack. To begin with, why would this person be targeted in the first place? Brainstorm possible scenarios:

1. A prosecutor is on trial in a high-profile murder case.
    a. In order to derail the case, the prosecutor is targeted for murder (kill one and the others may be less willing to carry on).
2. Prosecution of an organized crime boss.
    b. The killing of a prosecutor can frighten jury members as well as witnesses.
3. A district attorney takes a vocal stand against gangs, drugs, or corruption.

The second step is determining the process of the targeted attack. In other words, how would it be carried out?

1. Target identification: including some means of confirming identity, assuming the individuals tasked with carrying out the attack are not the ones ordering it. How would this be obtained?
2. Surveillance of the target to confirm residence location, routes traveled, vehicle identified, etc.
3. Reconnaissance of possible attack sites.

The third step is to identify the preattack indicators leading up to a hostile act that could be detected by the victim and/or protective personnel, such as:

1. People hanging around at the office and residence locations
2. Surveillance of vehicles, residences, and office
3. Informant information

Ideally, as well as assessing known groups, protective personnel should assess their own organization. Going back to the Risk Management Model, who would you most likely be called on to protect? Why would they most likely be targeted? As an example, what are the possible reasons to attack a prosecutor or judge?

1. Derail a case (kill one, others may walk away)
2. Revenge for a conviction
3. Revenge for a perceived "insult" by prosecutor
   a. Witness shuts up, disappears, "forgets"
   b. Jury members afraid
   c. Other prosecutors afraid
4. Personal, perhaps unrelated to profession

Conducting the "what if" analysis allows for protective personnel to plan in advance for the worst-possible-case scenario. By determining who in an organization is most likely to be targeted, coupled with possible attack scenarios, the protective unit will be better positioned to respond when information is developed on a possible targeted event.

THE "RED TEAM" ANALYSIS

This methodology was first developed by the U.S. military during the cold war to determine how bases were susceptible to attack. Teams referred to as "opposing forces" or OPFOR would conduct reconnaissance and surveillance, and plan and carry out a mock attack on a military installation. The goal was to test the base's responses to attack and the ability to repel the "enemy." Since then, the process of "red teaming" has expanded to many other areas of the government and the corporate world. The nature of red teaming makes an effective tool for protective operations.

This process seeks to replicate how a potential adversary would plan and carry out an attack on an individual. This, however, requires the participation of individuals with expertise in the group's methods of operation. For example, attacks carried out by an outlaw motorcycle gang can differ significantly from those carried out by street or prison gangs. The same holds true for mafia families and antigovernment extremists.

Many of the larger police departments and sheriff offices maintain intelligence, gang, narcotic, and/or organized crime units. These are the experts to consult with. The state and federal agencies monitor extremist organizations. They would/should be able to provide detailed information on the particular hostile organization's methods of operation. Provide these experts with the believed target of attack. Allow them to provide your team with details on how their "individual" group would operate on such a mission. If the method of attack includes a more specialized technique, such as a sniper or the use of explosives, then experts in these areas also should be brought into the fold to assist. Fortunately, most of the experts in these fields can be found in the larger agencies.

PREDICTIVE ANALYSIS

Predictive analysis has the goal of force protection (originating from the military, it refers to the protection of personnel of an organization) acquired by identifying threats and warns leaders of potential hostile actions in time to defeat or mitigate them.[12] It requires an analyst to use trends, historical events, and patterns in an effort to determine the probability of an attack. This can be exceedingly difficult as much of the required information is simply not available. While many of the described techniques are useful in assisting an analyst or organization in determining the potential of a threat against an individual, it cannot provide the information (short of informant-based information) of whether an attack is eminent.

If we operate with the assumption that the assassins will not vocalize a threat, then those assigned to threat assessment and/or protective operations need to focus on what is referred to as "the how,"[13] a term coined by STRATFOR (a Texas-based private intelligence corporation that provides businesses and individuals around the world with intelligence reports of current events, regional analysis, and potential regional threats).

> *Case in point:* On Sunday, November 10, 1974, members of the German Red Army Faction (RAF), aka the Baader Meinhof gang, a terrorist organization, assassinated a judge and president of the Berlin Supreme Court, Günter Von Drenkmann, at his home in Charlottenburg, Germany. This attack was perpetrated one day after RAF member Holger Meins died in prison. The RAF believing that Meins had been tortured and starved to death, sent out a four-man hit team in vengeance.[14] Less than three years later, on April 7, 1977, Chief Federal Prosecutor Siegfried Buback and his protective detail were assassinated by a two-person motorcycle hit team.[15] Buback had been actively involved in the investigation and prosecution of the Red Army Faction. During the subsequent claim of responsibility, the RAF indicated that the attack was in part due to the death of RAF member Ulrike Meinhof (who had committed suicide in prison on May 9, 1976), just a year earlier.

The timing of these two "revenge" attacks differed very significantly. While it would have been conceivable for authorities to ramp up security following the death of Meinhof, the passing of more than a year without incident undoubtedly led to a relaxing of the overall security posture. Therefore, the only effective method of predictive analysis in such a case is through knowledge of the attack cycle.

THE TARGETED ATTACK CYCLE

Organized targeted attacks are not generally hastily planned and implemented. Rather, they occur as a result of considerable conscious planning and effort. Once a hostile organization has decided to carry out an assassination or kidnapping, it presumably wants the operation to obtain the desired objective without loss or capture of its people and perhaps without identification of the group behind the attack. This is especially true of hits by criminal organizations and of course, hostile government agents.

The cycle of attack has been detailed by several different government and private agencies, all covering the same general process. All look at the cycle through the lens of the terrorist organization, which, given the current world situation, is understandable. However, for those individuals being targeted and their protective teams, the steps involved in the planning process may be reduced, considering the nature of the hostile organization (a criminal organization as opposed to a terrorist organization). Generally speaking, it is commonly accepted by the U.S. government that the terrorist planning cycle consists of seven steps[16]

1. Broad target selection
2. Intelligence and surveillance of potential targets
3. Specific target selection
4. Preattack surveillance, area and close target reconnaissance, and planning of the specific target and possible attack sites
5. Attack rehearsal
6. Actions on the objective
7. Escape and exploitation

For individuals assigned to threat assessment and/or surveillance detection, the best chances of determining a hostile presence is during steps 2 and 4, as these require a physical presence at some point. While step 5 obviously requires a physical presence and protective teams and individuals need to always practice good situational awareness, at the point of attack it is generally too late as the odds favor the attacker(s).

The first obvious step is the *selection of the target*. With terrorist and extremist organizations, the target has run the gamut from activists and local officials to heads of state. Many are also targets that have symbolic meaning or tend to bring notoriety to the group or cause. The search for targets has been documented repeatedly, perhaps most recently during the March 2, 2003, arrest of Nadia Desdemona Lioce by Italian authorities. A member of the latest generation of Italian Red Brigades, Lioce was on the run for the targeted killings of two Italian government officials. At the time of her arrest, she had in her possession a small digital camera as well as a list of prominent names, believed to be possible future targets.[17]

In instances when the hostile organization is a criminal group or a government agency, the individual is being targeted for a specific reason, either as a threat or a problem for the group. These two types of organizations have no need for symbolic strikes, nor need for media attention—in fact, quite the opposite. In these cases, the planning cycle will be reduced to just five steps and the potential for detection reduced down to two, with one of those being the attack itself. Regardless of the source of the threat, these targeting decisions are generally made at the command level of an organization. It is for this reason that it is very unlikely to come to the attention of authorities, at least initially.

The next stage is the *initial planning of the attack*. In the modern age, much of this can be performed via the Internet. If looking at a number of potential targets, the goal will be to select the one that offers the greatest chance of success. If only one has been selected, such as, for instance, a judge or mayor—deemed a problem to the hostile group—then the initial planning consists of determining if it is even possible to be successful. Ultimately, it will be those individuals that are deemed to be vulnerable, generally due to poor security measures and/or personal behavior patterns that are targeted.

Once the decision on a specific target has been made, a much more detailed planning process will ensue. Eventually, however, it will require some physical surveillance and reconnaissance to be made. Given that most hostile organizations targeting an official know where the victim works, that will be the logical starting point. From there, they will want to determine the residence location, routes of travel, frequented locations, etc. Most of this requires a person to be at these locations during the general time of movement. Each time a hostile surveillant goes out into the field, they become susceptible to detection.

The surveillance and reconnaissance may take a day, several days, or even several weeks. It is also during this time that the method of attack is determined or, at the very least, narrowed down to a couple of possibilities. The important part to remember is that this could be the last minute gathering of information before the rehearsal and attack.

Case in point: On December 20, 1973, Luis Blanco, then Prime Minister of Spain, was assassinated by the Basque terrorist group known as the ETA. The attack was perpetrated by detonating buried explosives as his vehicle passed over the top. During the subsequent investigation, it was discovered that the original plan had been to kidnap Blanco, but his protective detail was determined to be too professional and efficient. This resulted in the ETA terrorist group changing the plan into an assassination in which they used explosives to accomplish their goal.[18]

As part of the planning cycle, once the method of attack is determined, the necessary equipment needs to be obtained. Some are easy to acquire, while other components, such as explosives, can be harder to obtain and potentially compromise the operation. Additionally, vehicles are usually obtained, generally stolen a few days to a few weeks prior to the event date. Perhaps the most critical part of the planning is the location selected for the attack. For hostile organizations, the targeting of individuals offers several more ambush possibilities than would attacking a fixed structure. Statistically, attacks on individuals occur most often at the residence (32 percent of the time), followed by attacks during transit (30 percent of the time), and the office (14 percent of the time).[19] This statistic has a certain amount of logic in that the residence and routes of travel generally do not have the same level of security that one would find at an office environment. The issue for hostile surveillance teams is that there is an increased chance of being detected as suspicious and subsequently reported to authorities at these locations.

In some cases, rehearsals of the attack may be performed. Obviously, practice of the actual attack would be conducted at an isolated location. However, some onsite rehearsals can take place, such as the practice of escape routes and the initial arrival and setup. The next stage is the *execution of the operation*. The hostiles gather their equipment and deploy to the ambush staging area. Because they will want to limit their time at the ambush location to reduce potential compromise, they will position themselves for as short a period of time before the estimated arrival of the victim as possible. As they have planned the location, time, and type of attack, once at this stage, they will have the tactical advantage over the victim and protective detail.

As the victim enters the ambush location, the attack has essentially begun. Once it has been sprung, the only hope for survival is first and foremost the recognition of what is occurring, followed by a rapid implementation of an immediate action drill by either the victim or protective detail. In studies of human reaction time using police officers, it took an average of 1.82 seconds for an officer to draw his weapon from his holster, bring it to eye level, and fire a single round.[20] Given that this average was obtained by officers who were aware they were being timed and, therefore, ready, it is exceedingly likely that officers/victims reacting to an ambush situation would suffer a much greater delay. When this is coupled with the likelihood that the officer is in a suit, weapon concealed, with a seat belt on, the resulting delay could be such that the officer never has a chance to get into the fight at all.

Case in point: On June 12, 1999, at 12:52 p.m. in the afternoon, a friend and colleague of mine, Deputy Brad Riches, was on patrol and had stopped at a convenience store for coffee. Unknown to him, a man inside was armed with an AK-47 rifle just waiting to ambush any police officer who might come by. Upon seeing Deputy Riches pull up, the man stepped outside the store and opened fire, putting more than 24 rounds into the car and Deputy

Riches. He was never able to get his weapon out of his holster or even take off his seat belt before the attack was over and he had succumbed to his injuries.

The final stage is the escape and, in the case of terrorist organizations, the exploitation of the attack (which is beyond the scope of this work). Escape plans of the hostile force are a key element of any ambush, short of a suicide bombing attack, which obviously has no need/plan for escape. However, even in suicide attacks, there may still be other elements nearby that will need to make their escape. The route out of the ambush location must optimally allow for the hostile force to move rapidly with reduced chances of being detected and/or captured. While the escape is of little importance to a victim of an ambush, having the knowledge of the need can allow for a more concentrated and defined analysis of potential attack sites.

As a final case in point regarding varied and unknown threats stemming from hostile organized groups, comes the alleged targeting of Maricopa County Sheriff Joe Arpaio in Arizona in 2007. Information was developed by a credible informant that members of the local militia extremist group were attempting to hire some individuals linked to the Los Zetas organization to kill Sheriff Arpaio. The apparent goal of the killing was to outrage the public and make them more receptive to the desires of the militia.

While there has been wide dispute on the validity of the threat, what is known was that the informant was able to provide two pieces of information to validate his story. One was that the sheriff had recently dined at a local restaurant (which could have been just a coincidence) and the second, the amount of time it took Sheriff Arpaio to walk from his office to his vehicle had been determined (and later confirmed by authorities). This last piece of information is, in this author's mind, the most serious as it means that at least at some point, someone had been watching. Ultimately, authorities were never able to confirm the presence of the threat, even after spending over half a million dollars in providing protection.[21]

Short of detailed inside information, it will be exceedingly difficult to ever know or predict with absolute certainty if someone is being targeted. The key is awareness. Awareness of who operates in your area. Awareness of who your potential victim is or could be. Awareness of what your operational environment entails. Perhaps most important is your awareness of the targeted attack cycle. Finally, the worst sin in threat/risk assessments and protective operations is complacency. Just because something has or has not happened in the past does not mean it will be the same the next time around. Each and every threat must be carefully examined in its own right. To not do so could very well cost lives.

ENDNOTES

1. Hall, Allan (in Berlin), Pensioners 'Kidnap and Torture' Financial Adviser, June 23, 2009, www.telegraph.co.uk/news/worldnews/europe/germany/5612006/Pensioners-kidnap-and-torture-financial-adviser.html.
2. *Risk Management: An Essential Guide to Protecting Critical Assets* by the National Infrastructure Center, November 2002, 4.
3. Ndrangheta Mafia Explodes Bomb at Top Prosecutor's Home in Calabria by Steve Scherer, Bloomberg, August 26, 2010, www.bloomberg.com/news/print/2010-08-26/-ndrangheta-mafia-explodes-bomb-at-top-prosecutors-home-in-calabria,html.
4. Discussions with David Figueroa, a former mayor, senator, and a current Consul General of Mexico, described his personal dealings with the drug cartels of Mexico, including two assassination attempts. This process was also echoed in readings dealing with Sicilian mafias during the 1980s and the Colombian drug cartels of the 1990s. All of these organizations realize the heat that can result from an assassination on a government figure and find that it is cheaper in the end to buy those people that are problems.
5. Ibid.
6. Six Indicted for Novato Slaying by Tim Omarzu, *Novato Advance*, Wednesday, June 17, 2009, www.novatoadvance.com/articles/2009/06/17/news/doc.
7. Berton, Justin, Lizzard is a Rat, *East Bay Express*, www.eastbayexpress.com/news/lizard_is_a_rat/Content?oid=287961.
8. Pynchon, Marisa Reddy and Randy Borum, Assessing Threats of Targeted Group Violence: Contributions from Social Psychology, *Behavioral Science and the Law*, 339–355.
9. Ibid.
10. Parker, Susan P. *Murdered Judges Of the Twentieth Century and Other Mysterious Deaths*, Sunbelt Eakin, Austin, TX, 2004, 222.
11. McGovern, Glenn *Targeted Violence: A Statistical and Tactical Analysis of Assassinations, Contract Killings and Kidnapping*, CRC Press, Boca Raton, 2010, 305.
12. Developing a Predictive Capability in the Counterintelligence Integrated Analysis Center (CIIAC), Charles E. Harlan, *Military Intelligence Professional Bulletin*, 31, 1, January–March 2005, 18–23.
13. Vulnerabilities in the Terrorist Attack Cycle, STRATFOR, 9/29/2005.
14. WEST GERMANY: Guerrillas on Trial *TIME Magazine*, Monday, December 9, 1974, http://www.time.com/time/magazine/article/0,9171,908968,00.html.

15. West German Prosecutor Is Slain; Led Fight against Urban Guerrillas; Vilest Germany's Prosecutor Is Slain, *New York Times*, April 8, 1977, Page 1, http:// select.nytimes.com/gst/abstract.html?res=F60612FA3B5D167493CAA9178F D85F438785F9&scp=3&sq=Siegfried%20Buback%20assassinated&st=cse.
16. Surveillance Detection Training—Homeland Security attended by author.
17. Red Brigade Killers Given Life, *BBC News*, Wednesday, June 1, 2005, http:// news.bbc.co.uk/2/hi/europe/4601121.stm.
18. 1973: Spanish Prime Minister Assassinated, *On This Day*, BBC, http://news.bbc.co.uk/onthisday/hi/dates/stories/december/20/ newsid_2539000/2539129.stm.
19. McGovern, Glenn, *Targeted Violence*, p. 127.
20. Bumgarner, Jeffrey, William J. Lewinski, William Hudson, and Sgt. Craig Sapp, An Examination of Police Officer Chronometry: I Swear … I Don't Know How I Shot Him in the Back, The Scene: *The Journal of The Association for Crime Scene Reconstruction*.
21. Supposed Plot to Kill Arpaio is Doubted by Yvonne Wingett and Dennis Wagner, *The Arizona Republic*, October 7, 2007, http://www.azcentral.com/ arizonarepublic/news/articles/1007arpaio1007.html?&wired.

6

The Protective Advance

Today we were unlucky, but remember, we only have to be lucky
once, you will have to be lucky always.

Irish Republican Army

Whenever possible, before every protective operation, be it for the street-
level prostitute providing information on a local drug dealer, a judge over-
seeing an organized crime trial, even the president of the United States,
an advance site survey of the starting and ending locations along with
primary and secondary routes must be performed. In order for the survey to be conducted correctly, there are some critical items of intelligence
information that need to be obtained beforehand. This includes who the
principal will be, what the nature of the threat is (if known), the duration
of the operation, the starting and ending locations, and the approximate
times of pickup and arrival.

Unlike protective operations afforded to VIPs, such as celebrities, corporate executives, and dignitaries, when municipal- and county-level law
enforcement personnel are called in to provide protection, it is usually due
to the presence of a credible threat. This is exemplified by the types of individuals who commonly need to be protected by law enforcement agencies.
These principals generally fall into one of just a few categories: primarily
judges, prosecutors, department heads, victims, witnesses, informants,
and local elected officials, such as sheriffs, mayors, and city and county
council members. With the exception of perhaps the mayors of the larger
cities (who often do have some form of full-time police protection), most of
these individuals will not need a protective detail seven days a week, let

alone 24 hours a day. The exception to this would be for short periods of time, generally fixed around a court proceeding or while a specific threat is identified and investigated. On rare occasions, law enforcement members have been called upon to provide protection while a department official attends a public function; this occurs more often around election time. Those instances fall more into the realm of dignitary protection and are outside the scope of this book (however, see Chapter 12 for more detailed information regarding these types of operations).

Not having to deal with high-profile protective operations allows for a more focused examination of conducting types of advances involved in operations most likely to be encountered by law enforcement. These operations often consist of the pickup and transport of the principal from a residence to either court, the office, and back again with occasional meetings and perhaps lunch in between. They will range from one-time runs, to those lasting several months and longer depending on the circumstances. However, even on a one-time escort, a fair amount of time must be spent on preparing a quality protective advance. Recalling that the sole reason law enforcement has been asked to provide protection is because the person's life is believed to be in danger, not conducting a protective advance should be the exception to the rule. It is also important not to fool yourself into thinking you are a difficult target; just because you wear a badge and a firearm does not mean you have no need to worry about being attacked.

Case in point: On Tuesday, March 27, 2007, in Kiev, Ukraine, businessman Maksim Kurochkin was assassinated while in the custody of three police officers. Kurochkin was being escorted out of the courthouse after being advised he was to remain in custody in an extortion case. As the four men left the courthouse, a sniper positioned some 300 meters away in an 8th-floor room fired two rounds from a high-powered rifle. One of the rounds passed through Kurochkin and entered one of the police officers, injuring him.[1]

STATIC LOCATIONS

Once the initial intelligence information is acquired, the next phase is to obtain all available cyber-based information. The cyber threat (meaning information readily available about an individual such as address, upcoming meetings or events, photographs, etc.) to a potential victim cannot be overstated and includes routes of travel between the residence, office, and frequented locations. Before conducting the advance, the various mapping systems should be reviewed in order to determine what routes are already compromised. By performing this simple step, you acquire the knowledge a potential adversary may have about the operational area. This is not to say they cannot be used, but rather, this factor must be kept in mind when planning the routes to use. Additionally, aerial overheads of the starting and ending locations as well as potential ambush sites (once determined) should be acquired. Even if the area is familiar, an aerial image of the site will greatly assist in understanding the operational environment.

Whenever possible, before conducting the advance, the team members assigned the responsibility will need to obtain some sort of briefing on the nature of the threat. They should seek out as much information on the adversary—if known—as possible, at the very least, whatever is known about methods of operation and tactics. This knowledge will be key during the evaluation of locations and routes of travel. Obtaining this information may require reaching out to other experts outside your agency and the immediate area. Do not hesitate; if you do not have the answers, find someone who does.

A protective advance should be conducted by a minimum of two operators, who also will be on the protective team. While the advance can begin anywhere, it is easiest to start with the pickup point of the detail, most likely the residence. Use of a worksheet is beneficial and strongly encouraged to ensure thoroughness. The next stage involves going to all locations (even if it is your office) the detail will be visiting to evaluate the information about your adversary. Identify the hostile surveillance points (refer to Chapter 9 for more information) at each location, what routes are available immediately upon leaving the location, and how can they be changed. A word of caution: If it is a one-time run, then do not take the most direct route because an adversary, not knowing which way a target will take, may try and get lucky by positioning himself on the most likely route of travel. It is all too easy to be complacent about it and get sloppy, which is just what your adversary may be counting on.

When conducting the site survey, the focus should initially be on the most likely method of attack. This requires knowledge of who operates in your area and who is known or believed to be targeting your subject; in other words, the information generated from the threat/risk assessment. At each site, note where the entrances and exits (i.e., front doors, garages, gated parking areas, etc.) are located. What are their strengths and weaknesses, their construction, presence of locks, and in which direction do they open? What does the surrounding area look like, that is, does it have tall structures, dense vegetation, vacant lots, etc.? What cars are in the area, what is their condition, and where are they parked (this is not as important on one-time runs, but for extended details, it allows a team the opportunity to recognize a new vehicle to the area, which is potentially a threat)? Similar assessments will be conducted at each location to be visited.

In cases in which a safe house (apartment, home, motel/hotel) is used, a walkthrough of the grounds must be conducted. However—and this is a critical part of the advance—it must be determined if the agency has used the particular location before in similar circumstances. If so, the details of that operation must be obtained and reviewed for any potential conflict or compromise (see more on this in Chapter 7). Whatever the outcome, just as with an office and residence, site surveys of safehouse locations must be performed addressing the same questions.

IN TRANSIT

Between the starting and ending locations, it is necessary to identify routes of travel. At a minimum, there should be a primary and secondary route in each direction. What are the problem areas along the routes? Stop signs, natural choke points, such as hairpin turns and traffic circles, areas of known traffic congestion (depending on time of travel) all need to be identified. Which of these areas provide the adversary the optimal environment to attack (cover, concealment, place to stage, escape routes)? At these possible points of attack, what, if any, strengths are afforded the protective team? What is the quickest route to a police station, and to a hospital for each possible ambush location?

For protective details running for an extended period of time, more routes of travel between locations need to be identified. With each route, the previously mentioned questions/issues will have to be addressed. Perhaps more important will be the determination of possible routes for the final one-half mile into and out of a location. The criticality of this is due to the limited number of routes that can be used in and around the immediate vicinity of a residence, office, frequented location, etc. A competent adversary will recognize this and may try to take advantage of it.

As part of any advance, all routes need to be driven during the scheduled times of travel, making note of the duration of travel as well as other factors. In some cities, streets that are normally two way become one way, are closed, or in extreme circumstances even reverse direction during rush hours. Check with the local and state street and highway departments for street closures. When traveling through another jurisdiction, a point of contact should be made with that agency. A word of caution: If you are not familiar with the person or office, limit the information provided. Advise them of a law enforcement protective operation through their jurisdiction, and whether assistance is or is not needed. Obviously, more information sharing will be required if assistance is required (see Chapter 7). The goal is to limit the number of people with direct knowledge of the operation.

Contact numbers, including the local dispatch, should be obtained for all jurisdictions being traveled through (include the state patrol if highways will be traveled). This can be extremely important should a patrol officer with no knowledge of the nature of the motorcade attempt a traffic enforcement stop. The use of police traffic stop ruses, with devastating results for the victim, have been documented in the past. The decision on whether or not to stop must be discussed prior to the operation, hence, the point of contact and dispatch numbers (see Chapter 2 for more information on this topic).

> *Case in point:* On Sunday, November 3, 1996, in Tijuana, Mexico, former prosecutor Martin Ramirez-Alvarez was assassinated. The attack occurred as he was traveling with his wife, when a vehicle using police emergency lights conducted a traffic stop. Upon contact, Ramirez-Alvarez was dragged from his vehicle and shot six times at point-blank range.[2]

As part of the advance, specific points along routes of travel should be identified as checkpoints. These points are then given a codeword designation. This allows the motorcade to transmit its progress to the base of operations. By using the codeword, should anyone be monitoring the radio net (and you should always operate as though someone is), they will not be able to track you as easily. Perhaps more important, should radio contact be lost, the last call in would provide a starting point to send in help (to facilitate this, it is useful to determine the time of travel between checkpoints in order to give the base an idea of when a call-in is late). How these points are identified is obviously up to each unit. One thought for consideration is to use a code word for each possible ambush point. Whether used for identification of point of travel or for other additional reasons, it would allow for immediate identification of the attack site. This will enable a quicker response to an attack by reinforcements.

At each location identified as a potential ambush site (the residence, the office, frequented locations, and along the routes of transit—keeping in mind that there may be several points offering the right combination of ambush needs), a plan should be prepared for dealing with an attack at such areas. Questions that should be asked include:

- What method of attack does the site offer the best opportunity for?
- Should a protective detail motorcade be disabled, and what areas of cover and movement are available?
- What avenues of escape are there for the protective detail?
- What is the route to the closest trauma center from each possible ambush site?

The next part of the analysis is from the perspective of the adversary. Ideas of attack possibilities should be brainstormed among the team:

- What benefits does the location offer the attacking force?
- Does it allow for control of the target?
- Does it allow for the attackers to position themselves in advance with little to no chance of early detection?
- What method of attack that is known or believed to be part of the adversary's repertoire does the location support?
- How would an adversary most likely initiate the attack (this could be especially important if the adversary has a history of employing a ruse)?
- What avenues of escape does the location offer the adversary?

The areas around the pedestrian entrances/exits and vehicle pickup/ drop-off points of all visited locations should be thoroughly inspected. These need to be noted because the type of structure (i.e., columns, large art pieces, etc.), and dense vegetation could allow someone to wait and hide with the intention of striking from a close distance. A large number of targeted killings have occurred when a person was in the process of arriving or leaving a vehicle or building.[3] Given the substantial decrease in reaction time with attacks initiated at these points and the success rate, all of these areas must be documented.

Along the routes of travel, it is critical to identify those areas that restrict a vehicle, causing it to slow down and prevent a rapid escape. This can be as simple as a hairpin turn requiring a drastic reduction in vehicle speed (which should be avoided if at all possible) to more subtle aspects, such as an uphill gradient that would slow a vehicle down. One-way streets should be avoided, as well as construction zones, traffic circles, and the like, due to their constricting effects. In addition to one-way streets, small single-lane roadways should be avoided wherever possible, especially if vehicles are permitted to park on one or both sides of the roadway (Figure 6.1).

Figure 6.1 Driving down densely constricted roadways should be avoided if at all possible. The heavy pedestrian and vehicle traffic in conjunction with the restricted escape possibilities makes this a very dangerous road for a targeted individual to traverse.

These conditions would permit attackers to legally park along the route until the arrival of the motorcade. They could then easily pull out in an intercepting move, providing a quick and effective roadblock. This is even more of a threat if the perceived organization behind an attack could in any way employ an explosive device.

Signal-light-controlled intersections are potentially hazardous as they can force a motorcade to stop for a period of time. This provides an adversary with a stationary target, which is infinitely easier to attack over a moving one. However, short of a potential adversary having some sort of override, there is no way to control the said signal (there has only been one documented attack using such a device[4]). Lacking such a means, there is no way for the adversary to know with any certainty whether his target will catch the red light (and every delay in carrying out the attack increases the chance of detection). This chance, therefore, favors the protective detail. Stop signs and flashing red signals are a different story, as every vehicle is required to come to a complete stop. Given the large percentage of attacks on mobile targets at traffic control points,[5] detailed analysis of each should be made to determine which offer an adversary the greatest chances of success. Specifically, what is there about the intersection that could allow for a small hostile team to position itself for a short period of time without raising undue suspicions?

Case in point: On Thursday, March 16, 1978, the Italian Red Brigades carried out a highly coordinated attack on former Italian prime minister Aldo Moro. As was his routine, he left his home in his chauffeur-driven Fiat 130 en route to his church for morning Mass, which he attended every morning, prior to going to his office at Parliament. Along with a single bodyguard riding in the same car, there was a follow car with three police officers. As the small motorcade approached an intersection, a blonde woman standing nearby with a man waited for the right time to signal the start of the ambush. As Moro's car reached the intersection, a car pulled ahead and slammed on the brakes. As the male driver and female passenger got out, they pulled firearms consisting of at least one submachine gun and opened fired. At the same instant, four men dressed in Alitalia uniforms who had been standing at a bus stop at the intersection pulled out automatic weapons and opened fire on the three following police officers. Moro was successfully kidnapped and later killed.[6]

In addition to bus stops, what other features of the intersection provide an adversary cover for action? Is there a corner gas station that would allow someone to be out of their car awaiting the arrival of the target without anyone becoming suspicious? The potential cover possibilities can seem endless, but all need to be examined realistically for potential positioning of threats. Is there a corner café with outdoor seating, allowing for the monitoring of an intersection or portion of street (Figure 6.2)?

Case in point: On Tuesday, May 4, 1982, in Somerville, Massachusetts, the Honorary Turkish Consulate General, Orvile "Orhan" Gunduz, was assassinated by a lone gunman. The attack occurred as Gunduz was traveling through a construction zone that had caused a significant reduction in the speed of traffic. As Gunduz rounded a corner, a man approached and fired several rounds through the driver's window with a 9 mm pistol, striking him several times. The car drifted to a stop whereupon the killer pulled a .357 magnum revolver and fired a single round through Gunduz's ear at near point-blank range. In the subsequent investigation, the assassin was captured on CCTV sitting at a donut shop before the killing, having coffee and periodically looking at his watch.[7]

One key aspect when examining a potential ambush site is whether it offers good avenues of escape. The avenue of escape is an important issue for an adversary that can be easily overlooked by a protective detail. Except

Figure 6.2 Commercial areas, such as this, restrict a vehicle's speed while at the same time providing an adversary optimal cover for action, be it surveillance or staging for an ambush.

in cases of suicide bombings, every method of attack, be it a vehicle-borne improvised explosive device (VBIED), improvised explosive device (IED), or simple shooting requires a "way out."

> *Case in point*: On Monday, October 30, 2000, Supreme Court Judge Jose Lombardero, a judge in Madrid, Spain, was killed by a VBIED, along with his chauffeur and bodyguard, both of whom were police officers.[8] While the attack offered a number of lessons for investigators and protective personnel, one of the interesting factors was the proximity to a subway access point. The VBIED was remote-detonated, so it is entirely conceivable that the terrorists simply drove off in a vehicle, but escape by subway cannot be ruled out.

As part of the protective advance survey, key aspects of the surveillance detection process should be determined and incorporated. This is covered in greater detail in Chapter 9; for now, note that the advance should include the times most likely for hostile surveillance to occur as well as the positioning. While much more important for extended operations, surveillance detection should still be incorporated even in one-time details if for no other reason than it will help assist detection of a hostile scout advising his team positioned elsewhere of the departure. Identification of the possible hostile surveillance points at starting and ending points of the detail will serve the team well by reducing the areas that need to be observed when arriving at and departing from a location.

Here in the United States, we have been lucky, so to speak, with the level of sophistication of adversaries. For the vast majority of targeted attacks perpetrated over the past 100 years, firearms were the preferred method of attack.[9] However, with the recent wars in Iraq and Afghanistan and the documented instances of gang members receiving training and even taking part in combat operations, the likelihood of encountering a more tactically advanced adversary has greatly increased. When dealing with an adversary having the ability to attack by sniper or explosives, additional work must be incorporated as part of the advance.

SNIPER THREAT

If dealing with a potential sniper threat and if any of the starting and ending locations have overlooking structures nearby, there are a few factors that need to be taken into consideration. The first is the position of the shooter on or in the building. The sniper's level of training will often determine his most likely position. Roofs are generally avoided as the shooter's human form can easily be detected on the horizontal lines as well as being silhouetted against the skyline.

That said, roofs have been used in the past and, therefore, can never be dismissed outright. Within the structure itself, a sniper could position himself behind any window that provides a view of the target. An easy way to identify the location of a sniper in a building if he has been spotted, is by way of an alphanumeric system. Looking at a structure, the top row of windows would be labeled one. The next level would be two, and so on. The ground floor should be labeled "ground" and the top of the structure "roof." Each window of a given floor is then labeled with a letter beginning on the left and working to the right. This allows any operator who can see a threat to quickly dial in the rest of the team as to the sniper's probable location.

The distance between all possible sniper nests and potential points of entrance/exit and arrival/departure points should be noted. This should also include calculations for the potential high-angle attack nests. This calculation allows one to determine the exact distance between the rifle and the target (any current or former military or SWAT sniper can provide the formula). This is important to understand, as while the building may be only 100 meters away, the actual distance, because of the angle, may be farther. While generally the distance change is only small, depending on the weapon system being employed by the protective detail, it can still make all the difference. Ideally, if faced with such a threat, a trained sniper should be brought in to assist the advance site survey.

One method of planning for a sniper threat is by way of what I refer to as a "reverse range card." Traditionally, range cards are prepared by military units anytime they are going to be defending a fixed location for an extended time. Snipers make extensive use of range cards for a variety of reasons. The cards help the sniper ensure that he has completely scanned an area of responsibility for all landmarks, avenues of approach, possible enemy locations, and positions of cover. It also helps him document the range and elevation estimates to each of these areas, which will assist him and his assistant in the heat of the fight. In a targeted attack, it stands to reason that a sniper, needing to concentrate on only a couple of exit/ entrance points to a structure, will plot potential points of cover a protective team might move to in the event he misses the first shot.

By preparing the reverse range card, the individuals conducting the site survey also are forced to scan the area for potential targets, or in this case, sniper nests in which a sniper might likely position himself. Regardless of whether one is facing a trained sniper team or an individual with a hunting rifle, by having taken the time in advance to scan the area and identify possible hostile positions, the team gains two advantages. First, during the actual running of the protective detail, the number of areas to be immediately aware of and scanned, at least initially, is reduced. Second, should the team be engaged from one of these locations, it would rapidly know which of their weapon systems to employ in order to deal with the threat, as the distances would already be known.

Case in point: On Wednesday, March 12, 2003, at approximately 12:30 p.m., the then prime minister of Serbia, Zoran Djindjic, was assassinated as he left his vehicle just outside of the Parliament building in Belgrade. As Djindjic stepped out of his vehicle to cover the approximately 10 feet to the doorway of the building, in the company of his protective detail, a sniper positioned inside another building approximately 360 feet away fired two rounds in rapid succession. Both rounds found their mark, striking Prime Minister Djindjic and killing him.[10] While the protective team was armed with submachine guns and pistols, the distance the sniper fired from was well beyond the range of those weapons to effectively respond to the threat.

109

Ideally, if facing a real and legitimate sniper-based threat, a tactic whose effectiveness has been proved time and time again, a protective team must take precautionary measures beyond what it might normally do. This could include moving the visit to a location in another less vulnerable area. Arriving on another side of a structure can provide effective shielding from a sniper threat. Employment of counter sniper teams or teams of operators at locations judged attractive for a sniper to position himself in should be considered. Finally, if all else fails, get the vehicle as close to the structure as possible and move very quickly, but sporadically.

THREATS FROM EXPLOSIVES

Improvised explosive devices (IEDs) present a major problem for individuals and protective details. Whether cached inside a vehicle parked on the side of the road or hidden in debris, the destruction these devices cause is often devastating. In dealing with explosive-based attacks, the key to survival is distance and shielding. Unfortunately, in the urban environment, unarmored vehicles (and occasionally, even armored ones) do not provide effective shielding within a distance of between two to nine feet from a detonation site that has a minimum safe distance recommendation of 500 to 1500 meters.

Vehicle-borne improvised explosive devices, VBIEDs in the common vernacular, can hold between 100 and 1000 pounds of explosive material with little to no visible signs, if constructed correctly. VBIEDs containing between 500 and 1000 pounds of explosives can have a lethal blast pressure out to between 100 and 125 feet traveling between 3,300 and 29,900 ft/s from the detonation site. Given that most city street lanes average about nine foot wide, even a four-lane roadway, the equivalent of approximately 36 feet wide, easily falls within the lethal range. This has, of course, been proved repeatedly with tragic effects. Even IEDs ranging between 25 and 50 pounds of explosive material can cause major damage in an area out to 12 feet from the blast site.

VBIEDs—even if provided suspension reinforcement—if loaded with a large amount of explosive material may be detectable by those searching for such a vehicle. However, the problem for protective details is that terrorists are often aware of this, and as a result position the VBIEDs among other vehicles parked on the side of a street. Terrorists also have historically placed these devices relatively close to the starting and ending locations (residence or office). The advantages this offers the bombers are that these areas characteristically have a limited number of avenues of approach as well as a large number of legitimately parked vehicles. Even when practicing good security by changing travel routes, all will be constrained by the environment to close the final distance by taking one of perhaps fewer than four ways in. Additionally, these areas, due to the heavy pedestrian traffic, tend to have much slower speed limits, as well as heavier traffic during the rush hours, all of which aid in concealment and timing.

While these areas of possible attack have always been of concern for protective teams, when dealing with an explosive-based threat, the danger potential increases exponentially. As history has documented, explosive-based targeted attacks have occurred in areas that constrain vehicles to slow down and also permit the device to be concealed. Primarily, this means traffic intersections that allow vehicles to be parked in close proximity to the corners, more specifically, near intersections with stop signs and where the target is known to make a turn.

The key to all explosive devices used in targeted attacks is correctly timing the triggering. Trigger the device too soon or too late and the target could be out of the kill zone. For vehicle motorcades, the greater the speed of travel, the more difficult it is to correctly time the device for maximum effect. It is for this reason that hostile organizations employing explosive devices tend to position them at locations where the motorcade will be constrained by the environment to slow down. The use of marks or indicators near the attack site has been documented as having been employed by terrorist organizations to assist in correctly timing the triggering of the device.

On smaller secondary streets, in addition to parked vehicles, IEDs could be concealed in trash bins, debris, or other containers.

Case in point: On July 14, 2006, in Tskhinvali, Republic of South Ossetia, an IED was concealed in a hollow tree trunk and was detonated as the target was in the process of entering his vehicle.[11] The target, Bala Bestauty, a commander of a Special Forces unit, was injured in the attack.

While rarer in occurrence than VBIEDs, explosives have been effectively deployed and detonated in such locations against a motorcade target. Explosives also have been found under bridges, but this threat largely depends on the construction and age of the bridge. With most modern bridges, at least in the United States and Canada, short of an enormous amount of explosives, this threat remains extremely low.

In the end, regardless of an individual's position within the protective unit—operator or analyst—both need to study the modus operandi of their potential adversaries. Obtaining and updating knowledge of how hostile organizations operate allows the protective unit to perform its functions in a more expedient and effective manner. This can be critical when conducting a protective advance survey and especially important during preparation for last-minute protective details.

ENDNOTES

1. Ukraine: Kyiv Assassination Leaves Trail of Intrigue by Roman Kupchinsky, March 29, 2007, Radio Free Europe, www.rferl.org/content/article/1075578. html.
2. Former Prosecutor in Mexico Gunned Down by Anne-Marie O'Connor, *LA Times* staff writer, November 15, 1996, www.articles.latimes.com/1996-11-15/news/mn-65016_1_federal-prosecutor.
3. McGovern, Glenn, *Targeted Violence: A Statistical and Tactical Analysis of Assassinations, Contract Killings and Kidnappings*, CRC Press, Boca Raton, FL, 2010.
4. Ibid., p. 82.
5. Ibid., p. 123.
6. 1978: Aldo Moro Snatched at Gunpoint, *BBC On This Day*, www.news.bbc. uk/onthisday/hi/dates/stories/march/16/newsid_4232000/4232691.stm.
7. Vehicle Attacks, Orvile Gunduz, PraesidiaDefense, www.praesidiadefense. com/welcome/Press_and_publications_on_terr/vehicle_attacks/vehicle_ attacks.html.
8. Aznar Defiant after 'ETA-style' Bombing, October 30, 2000, cnn.com www. archives.cnn.com/2000world/Europe/10/30/spain.blast.05/.
9. McGovern, *Targeted Violence*.
10. Serbs Premier Is Assassinated; Led in Reform by Daniel Simpson, March 13, 2003, *The New York Times*, World, www.nytimes.com/2003/03/13/world/ servs-premier-is-assassinated-led-in-reform.html.
11. Georgia and South Ossetia on the Brink of New War by Vladimir Novikov, Tbilisi; Gennady Sysoev, July 15, 2006, Kommersant, www.kommersant. com/page.asp?idr=18id=690269.

7

Operational Security (OPSEC)

We know what it takes to assure victory and preclude surprise.
We must look at our own operations in light of these principles
because without a doubt our adversaries do.

John Major Davis
(U.S. Army Ret.)

Consider the following scenario: An agency has been tasked with moving
an informant from his present location at a safe house to court and back
again. The informant is a senior member of a large semiorganized criminal gang who is testifying against another gang member in order to beat
his own narcotics violation case. It is believed that the gang is aware of
the betrayal and has given the "green light" for the informant to be killed.
The protective unit accomplishes the mission without a hitch. Does this
sound familiar? It is probably carried out on a routine basis throughout
the United States.

Fast-forward a year or two later and a similar scenario occurs.
However, unbeknownst to the protective detail, that former "informant"
is now back in the gang, but in order to get back in the good graces of his
gang, he provided detailed information about your team. The gang now
knows what entrance your team used to access the main courthouse. They
know the one or two routes that were traveled, what cars were used, the
makeup of the team, possibly even weapons and equipment utilized, and,
of course, the hotels, motels, or safe houses used for overnight stays—all

very critical information that anyone planning an attack on a protected individual would pay handsomely for. All this information your team provided merely by doing their job. In the world of protective operations, only law enforcement and intelligence agencies generally have to deal with such operational compromise.

The reality is that this scenario is not that farfetched. Further, it does not have to be this elaborate. It just as easily could be a street-level prostitute testifying against some local pimp or drug dealer. Protection is provided to the prostitute who is later linked to an opposing gang to that of an informant that the agency protective detail is now assigned to. The point is, unlike in traditional police, SWAT or military operations, keeping a unit's tactics and equipment secret concealed, to the extent possible, is relatively easy to accomplish; only in protective operations is an outsider able to view all first hand. This becomes a problem when the protected individual is a criminal and/or linked to people of dubious character.

A critical aspect of protective operations, especially for those run on the more discreet level, is maintaining operational security, more commonly referred to as OPSEC. It is defined by the Operations Security Professional's Association as "an analytic process used to deny an adversary information—generally unclassified—concerning friendly intentions and capabilities by identifying, controlling, and protecting indicators associated with planning processes or operations." So what does this mean? OPSEC is a tool, a process by which a protective unit examines itself through the eyes of an adversary in order to determine what can be learned about a unit (just as one would in evaluating vulnerability of a protectee). This is generally performed by watching the unit's activities during operations and training. Hence, if a protective unit employs good OPSEC, they control the amount of information an adversary can easily collect. More importantly, they understand what aspects of their methods of operation should be considered compromised.

The goal then is to take a hard and thorough look to identify the unit's vulnerabilities. What information would an adversary be able to collect about your unit that could be exploited at a later date? OPSEC is commonly broken down into a five-step process or cycle. What a unit will quickly discover is that the steps are very similar to what they would normally perform for their protectee. The difference here is that they will perform it upon themselves. The individual steps are as follows:

1. *Identification of critical information.* As part of OPSEC, you need to have a complete understanding of what the adversary most likely already knows. Critical information includes:
   a. Any open source information, regardless of whether or not the adversaries have the perceived sophistication. This is the easiest place to start.
   b. What the adversary needs to know to be successful. This can assist in identifying aspects of a team's operations that could be susceptible.
   c. Where the adversary is likely to look to obtain needed information.
2. *Threat analysis.* As discussed in Chapter 5, this process can be difficult when the hostile organization representing the threat is not known.
   a. If you do not know the adversaries, how will you know what they are targeting? If you do not know their target, how will you know what to protect? This goes back to understanding who is in your area of operations.
   b. *The threat.* A combination of who the adversary is and what they want to accomplish. Do they have the intent and capability?
   c. An important factor to consider is detailed in Richard Heuer's work *The Psychology of Intelligence Analysis* (APO, 1999): "Intelligence analysts should be self-conscious about their reasoning processes. They should think about how they make judgments and reach conclusions, not just about the judgments and conclusions themselves."
3. *Vulnerability analysis.* Analyze your team and your protectee's vulnerabilities. This needs to be a hard look as though you were going to carry out the attack. What information can be quickly determined about the team and what could be determined over an extended period (refer to Chapter 5 for more information).
4. *Risk assessment.* How likely is it that the protective detail will be attacked during an operation? A great deal of this depends on the adversary (refer to Chapter 5 for more information).
5. *Application of countermeasures.* As the vulnerabilities are identified, an adversary could gain an understanding of the methods and inner workings of a unit; steps must be taken to prevent the compromise to the degree possible.

OPSEC applies to all levels of protective operations. Complacency in the form of routine, habits, laziness, and overconfidence is the enemy of

OPSEC. OPSEC analysis of a unit needs to include their normal operational methodology. It also should include routines followed by protective details in preparation for an operation. Surveillance detection teams need to make sure their OPSEC is solid. (Patience is perhaps the most important aspect of OPSEC while on surveillance detection).

> *Case in point:* A perfect example of this can be found in the aforementioned attack on Magistrate Falcone in Sicily on May 23, 1992. Members of a mafia hit team had Falcone's home under surveillance. More precisely, they had his armored car under surveillance. When they noted the arrival of a police officer to pick up the car, they notified their command structure. When this was coupled with the information coming from the hostile surveillance of Falcone in Rome during his travel to the airport, the hit team could be reasonably sure Falcone was coming to them.[1]

This thought pattern of watching the protective detail members was more recently suggested by Ali Mohamed, the man behind the bombings of the U.S. embassies in Africa and the trainer of the personal bodyguards of Osama bin Laden (OBL). Ali Mohamed provided this information to the United States government at the request of a Delta Force commander.[2] Mohamed stated that one could almost never find OBL, but you could find the bodyguards, and it was likely that they would be less careful and that by focusing on them and their families, all that was needed was patience and OBL would fall into their hands. While this was never played out to see if Mohamed was correct, the logic is solid. This should give anyone assigned a protective function cause to think of their own actions. Have they subconsciously fallen into a pattern that could be detrimental to an operation?

COUNTERINTELLIGENCE

A critical component of OPSEC is counterintelligence or CI. The purpose of CI is to detect, identify, assess, counter, neutralize, and ultimately exploit an adversary's intelligence collection efforts. While it might be easy for a law enforcement agency to dismiss a potential for a hostile intelligence presence, as Lawrence Sulc wrote in his book *Counter Intelligence for Law Enforcement* (Varro Press, 1996): "When facing international organized crime groups, terrorist organizations and drug cartels, you are facing hostile intelligence." The most recent example of this can be found in Mexico.

The Los Zetas drug cartel is known to employ a group of individuals called the Falcons. Comprised of both male and female operatives, they are tasked with the monitoring of and intelligence collection on rivals, military, and all levels of law enforcement operating in their territory. It has been reported by various sources that the Falcons employ sophisticated surveillance equipment and techniques, and perhaps even have wiretap capabilities (skills the Sicilian mafia was believed to possess in their heyday). While perhaps not the norm for most criminal organizations, it is vitally important to keep in mind that the adversary may have a better intelligence apparatus than you. Certainly, if the threat stems from environmental, racial, and religious extremists, as well as biker gangs and some organized crime groups, then hostile intelligence gathering must be assumed as having occurred.

By way of example, during a briefing on outlaw motorcycle gang (OMG) members in the local area, it was mentioned that a member of a notorious OMG had been contacted at a residence in the company of a female adult who had been wearing an identification badge indicating she worked for the crime lab. After the briefing, I inquired if any follow-up had been conducted, as the crime lab was part of my organization. I was surprised to hear that he was not aware of any further follow-up. Fortunately, he was able to provide me with the address where the contact had been made. In a short amount of time, I was able to identify the woman in question as well as relatives, all of which were checked against the list of crime lab employees. Fortunately, the OMG-linked member did not work for the crime lab; however, I did discover that the woman worked for the same agency as the officer that conducted the presentation. This information was subsequently forwarded to that individual. I can only hope that it was acted on.

The counterintelligence aspect of OPSEC includes the manipulation of information obtained by the adversary. While beyond the scope of this work, suffice it to say that providing false information about a protective operation can provide an increased degree of protection. If this aspect of CI is to be employed, it requires a considerable amount of active participation by the protective unit and the law enforcement intelligence unit.

Information gathered by a hostile entity is extremely dangerous to your protectee and team. Unfortunately, given the nature of the job, there is little that can be done to prevent it outright. What can be done is to monitor each protective operation with respect to what was carried out in regards to each individual. This is especially the case with subjects involved with state witness protection programs. These individuals are in a position to obtain a wealth of information in a short period of time.

If they eventually fall out of the program, they still have the intelligence (see Figure 7.1.).

One of the first things that should be performed upon law enforcement's initial receipt of threat information is to determine the victim/target's OPSEC. Some of this information will be useful later during the vulnerability assessments. Some of the questions, however, differ from habits and routes of travel and times of arrival and departure. I have found the best place to start is, again, with the target/victim's vehicle.

The first question is, the location of the parked vehicle. For some office/department heads, they may have assigned parking (hopefully it is not labeled with a name or rank/position, but this is still common). If not assigned, is it parked in or very near to the same general location that they park at everyday? (Most times, as is the human habit, the answer is yes.) As you approach, what does it say about the owner? Is it secured, doors locked, and windows up? Are there personal license plates and/or plate frames that provide an indication of what that person does for a living? Is there any type of sticker required for parking affixed to the car that identifies a specific employer or location? While this may not be important in a sea of cars with similar stickers, it can be critical once the vehicle is later parked at a residence. It may be all the adversary needs to confirm the location of the target. Is there a license plate and/or frame indicating the owner's profession or identity?

In addition to parking stickers, other items in the interior, such as documents, books, periodicals, photos—anything providing identification of the person's profession, residence, work place, etc.—can be a great place for potential compromise. Speaking of stickers, there is a certain set that has become more and more common that provides a fair amount of information with a quick glance. These stickers are the little figures detailing the family make-up to include even the presence of dogs. Some of these even provide the names of the individual family members. Should any potential targets be found with these on their car, they must be strongly encouraged to remove them. The list can be endless, so when looking at the car what I liked to do is to approach the vehicle as though I only have a notion that the car belongs to my target and, therefore, I am looking for anything that can provide confirmation.

As with everything, there is a dark side—in this case, bad OPSEC. It includes specialized equipment visible on a person or vehicle, be it a badge or the bulge of a poorly used concealed weapon holster. Police indications including vehicles, wire radio gear, etc.—all can compromise you. It only takes one operative with bad OPSEC to blow the whole team

OPSEC Chart of Operations

Date	Name	Organization	Vehicles Used	Weapons	Team Members	Locations	Routes
2/12/2010	John Doe	Southside Locos	Silver Crown Vic	Side arms	Team A	Hotel A and main court	See route notes
4/23/2010	Jane Doe	Ridge Runners (OMG)	Green Taurus	Side arms, M-4s	Team A and B	Hotel B and main court	See route notes
8/2/2010	Mike Smith	Local street dealer	Silver Crown Vic	Side arms	Team B	Hotel C and drug court	See route notes

FIGURE 7.1 This simple chart details the date, name, gang links, cars used, weapons employed and that could have been seen, team members used, locations, and routes traveled.

and operation. Every individual on a team must behave normally—that is, in line with the cover for action. Cops can be notorious for having bad OPSEC; it therefore is wise for team members to examine each other.

If an adversary witnesses possible protective team members getting into personal vehicles with law enforcement-related decals, what information does it provide? At a minimum, it indicates the individuals have probably no concept of operational security. If the decals indicate military, SWAT, or the like backgrounds, it can alert the adversary they are facing a more aggressive, motivated, and, more specifically, a better-trained operative. Perhaps more to the point, it could cause an adversary to opt to want to remove such an individual prior to ambushing a protective detail.

Another often-encountered OPSEC problem when dealing with threats is a response procedure that is inherently common. In some organizations, if a threat is deemed credible enough, the targeted victim is allowed to park closer to the office. By doing this, however, a potential target has now lost a certain amount of protection by way of anonymity, as they will now park in a "known" location allowing for easier identification, confirmation, and targeting by an adversary. In this case, the protective security measure has become a liability. It is similar to the scene in the Hollywood movie *Die Hard* where the terrorists wait for the arrival of the FBI and for them to follow the standard operation procedures of shutting down the power to the building, thereby allowing for the vault security features to be bypassed. If an adversary is aware of your agency's SOP (standard operating procedure) in responding to threats, your potential targeted victim could be in severe danger as your adversary is most likely very sophisticated.

ROUTES AND ADVANCE PLANNING

Operational compromise also can be a result of the Internet, more specifically, the various mapping and imaging sites. Equally important can be the advertisement of locations that a principal will be in the future. Whenever planning a protective movement, it is vitally important to know what is already "known" or could be about your protectee. While keeping in mind that the vast majority of attacks have occurred at the start or ending destinations, it is equally important not to provide an adversary with additional possibilities for ambush by traveling the same routes between said locations.

A good starting point then is to run the beginning and ending locations of a detail through the various mapping sites. Often these provide the easiest and most direct routes between locations. This is not to say these routes cannot be used, only realize that there is a great potential for them to be "known" and, therefore, they should be considered operationally compromised. By having the knowledge of what an adversary may reasonably be expected to know about—in this case, a route of travel—allows the planner the ability to "tweak" the routes in such a way to potentially regain the element of surprise.

This also brings up another issue of operational compromise that is inherent with protective details over an extended period. While more likely to be encountered by corporate security teams dealing with CEOs and the like, it can conceivably be an issue for some in law enforcement, should a mayor, judge, or elected official request a long-term protective detail. The issue is that, between two locations such as the residence and the office, there are only so many different routes that can be traveled. The same is true for the times of travel.

These extended duration protective operations afford the adversary the luxury of extending the amount of time spent in surveillance and reconnaissance of the target, thus potentially reducing his/her continued presence over the short term and through the use of associates, thereby decreasing the potential for their detection. At the same time, this allows for the adversary to gain much more operational intelligence on the protective detail and the target. Any potential lapses in operational security by the protective team can lead to advantages given to the adversary. Thus, it is critical in such long-term operations that the team be keenly aware of the compromise potential, that they track their tactics, equipment, and techniques used, and that they make the most potential of guile and subterfuge in order to maintain safety.

SAFE HOUSES

When dealing with witnesses/victims, a choice that often is required is to physically move them out of their current residence to ensure their safety. Primarily, this can be due to the close link between witnesses and defendants. Assuming the witness/victim follows the rules and refrains from contacting friends and relatives by phone, in person, on social networking sites, etc., then the use of safe houses are generally just that—safe.

The problem that can arise is if law enforcement gets lazy and drops the ball, thereby putting that witness/victim in danger. Most agencies do not rent or own a selection of safe houses within their jurisdictional limits and/or the immediate surrounding area. Beyond the economic burden this entails, it is actually better from an operational standpoint not to. Hotels, motels, travel lodges, and the like are most often used as safe havens for witnesses/victims, allowing the individual to hold up at least initially in a safe manner until a more suitable arrangement can be made. The beauty these establishments offer is, first and foremost, the sheer number of them (at least in the mid-size to large population centers). This allows for a victim/witness to be housed in any one establishment for however long it is deemed necessary. In a location like the San Francisco Bay Area of California, with some 10 counties and their accompanying cities all within a hour or less drive, the anonymity these possibilities provide is enormous.

The problem that can often develop is when law enforcement agencies drift unknowingly into their own habits and routines that result in compromise the moment a witness is housed. When a certain location is "cop friendly," it makes it all the more easily to fall into the habit trap. What I am referring to is using the same locations repeatedly as safe houses. This is not saying good locations cannot be used more than once. The fact is that some offer the perfect combination of ease of use, safety, and security, etc. The key is to remember that a particular location is compromised the moment it is used. There is no way to ensure the victim/witness will not tell another about what happened and where they stayed.

Let us face it, even though at the time of the protective operation the victims/witnesses were frightened and in perhaps fear for their very life, later on when the danger has subsided, it makes a great story to tell friends. Right out of a movie, it will come up, and things such as places stayed, team makeup, vehicles, route, etc., will get out. Since there is no way of knowing for sure if the former protectee has talked or not, the team needs to operate as though it has been compromised

The use of houses/locations—be it an actual house/apartment or hotel room (here after referred to as safe house)—needs to be monitored. This is especially true for those agencies that could or do provide protection to witnesses, victims, or informants. Obviously, depending upon the nature of the case, these individuals could range from fine, upstanding citizens to prison gang members. Regardless, any time an individual is housed temporarily, that safe house needs to be considered compromised. In the case of hotels/motels, it is all too easy to fall into the trap of repeated use. These locations like the business and, therefore, many will take extra steps to make obtaining rooms as painless as possible. This relationship should be used to the benefit of all, but it should not be repeatedly used in a way that increases the danger to the protectee.

Ideally, it would be beneficial to have a list of 10 or more motels/hotels within the county that could be used for overnight stays (in addition to any traditional safe houses an agency might have access to). A simple spreadsheet like the example shown in Table 7.1 would list the date, name, location, case, and any gang links for each person housed overnight. Any future housing would be compared to the list to determine any conflicts. This is more apt to arise in cases involving gang members. For example, an agency houses a "red" gang member for a case. The operation goes as planned without issue. Several months later, the agency is housing a "blue" or opposing gang member in a case involving the "reds." That "red" gang member, now back or trying to get back in the good graces of his gang, recalls where he was kept overnight—you get the picture.

Remember, the protective unit should have the final word on housing a protectee. Never let accountants decide on a location, as that is a sure way to get a person killed. One final note: With hotels/motels as part of the OPSEC for safe houses, the reservations and payments should be made via undercover identification and credit cards.

TEAM AND TEAM MEMBER OPSEC

Beyond the team, each individual has a responsibility to practice excellent OPSEC. To begin with, one should never ever talk about a protective operation, but especially in front of or to nonteam members. Discussion among team members is not an issue, discussion with a spouse, while not advised is still not much of an issue. However, discussions out in the open should never occur. While the chances of someone overhearing you and knowing what you are talking about is very remote, it has happened and in this deadly game, the risks are too great.

The use of human engineering has been used by terrorists, criminals, and intelligence agents, even those practicing corporate espionage. While most of us will never have to face such an adversary, if you practice employing good OPSEC now, it will become a habit. As an example, in 1998 I had the opportunity to assist members of a U.S. army intelligence unit conduct their final exercise prior to their being allowed to go operational. Several local detectives and I were asked to maintain a close proximity to our targeted intelligence officer in order for us to overhear a conversation with the "contact" (played by the instructor). Inside of a local café and armed only with a newspaper and a cup of coffee, I was just another face in the crowd, going about my business. As a result, I was able to overhear a good portion of the conversation, which was later told to the intelligence officer (much to his chagrin). The intelligence officer later stated he thought I was taking a long time to read the paper (*always* trust your instincts).

OPSEC extends also to the weapons and equipment. If it does not have to be exposed, then don't! The nature of protective operations at all levels requires a need to take advantage of being covert. As part of the operational security, a person and a team should not let the types of weapons and equipment normally deployed with them, or that they have access to, become common knowledge. This especially includes the number of rounds or "combat load" that a team member carries while operational.

When transporting an individual of dubious character, if heavier weapons are deemed necessary, they should be held in one of the follow cars, out of sight. If it is decided that one operator with the protectee is to be armed with such a weapon, it should be something readily concealable, such as the Heckler and Koch MP-5K. This way, unless the motorcade is attacked, the protectee never sees the weapon systems a team has available. If attacked, then who cares what is seen?

As with individual OPSEC, the team also must be monitored. This is especially the case in longer-term operations. Teams can fall into their own "patterns," which is obviously problematic. Teams must monitor their *signature*, such as:

- The number of vehicles generally employed (including make, model, etc.)
- The number of operatives deployed as well as their disbursement in the motorcade
- Routes of travel taken between fixed locations (i.e., office and court, the jail, city hall)
- Common starting locations (meaning the arrival and departure areas at an office or frequented location, such as a courthouse)

All this information must be logged, tracked, and monitored, along with the nature/source of the threat and the nature of the victim/witness. Only through this analytical process will a team ensure OPSEC is preserved to the maximum extent possible.

While good OPSEC is critical to an individual and a team, by itself it is not always enough, hence, the need for situational awareness and surveillance detection.

Case in point: On Thursday, June 8, 2000, at approximately 7:15 a.m. in Athens, British Military Attaché Brigadier Stephen Saunders was assassinated by members of the November 17 terrorist organization. The brigadier was no stranger to danger, having spent time in Northern Ireland during the Troubles and as such, he had taken steps to maintain a low profile. He was driving his white Rover with local plates and no external markings indicating any connection to the British embassy. On the morning of the attack, he was traveling from his residence to the embassy and was stuck in the normal morning traffic congestion. As he approached an intersection within approximately two miles of the embassy, a motorcycle with two riders approached and opened fire with a .45 caliber pistol. Brigadier Saunders was struck four times and died at the scene.[3]

SITUATIONAL AWARENESS

Situational awareness is simply defined as "being aware of what is occurring in your immediate area and, in particular, identifying potential threats in advance so they can be avoided." However, it is a mindset that must be practiced and, more importantly, can be employed by any individual regardless of their tactical background. Walking down a sidewalk all the while looking only at the ground, or eyes staring at the latest portable tech gadget is a sure way to be ignorant of a threat until it is upon you.

Unfortunately, in society there are many dangers. Through situational awareness many of these can be avoided if they are detected early enough. This is not about being paranoid every time you leave your house or office, or whether an individual is brave or a coward, it is about preventing a hostile situation from occurring to you, your family, your protectee, and your team. An important part of situational awareness and operational security is knowing your capabilities and your weaknesses.

When I speak to groups and individuals on providing for their own security, I explain that anytime they are out with the family, their vulnerability to dangerous situations increases substantially. This is because, when they are alone, when the first signs of danger are detected, they can move away rapidly or deal with the threat head on if there is no avoiding it. When family members are present, the individual must attempt to maneuver the family to a safe location discreetly. If by circumstances they are forced to deal with a threat and the family is around, if the threat is multiple adversaries, the family's presence could conceivably be used against them. I further demonstrate this by stating that it doesn't matter if you are armed and extremely well trained in hand-to-hand combat, adding that most police agencies tell their officers that in off-duty situations it is better to be a good witness than to take enforcement action.

An excellent example of this occurred many years ago and was used by some agencies to demonstrate the need to avoid hostile encounters when off-duty. The case involved an off-duty police officer who was going to the store with his daughter. At some point upon their arrival, while still in the parking lot, the officer recognized a robbery in progress. The officer decided to take enforcement action, hid his daughter near a vehicle, and took on the robbers. Unfortunately, the robbers had seen the daughter and decided that killing her was the best way to cause the officer to break off his engagement. The tactic worked with extremely tragic results.

Therefore, situational awareness as part of operational security is understanding your current abilities, weaknesses, and strengths, coupled with maintaining an awareness of surroundings. There are many different methods of codifying this awareness, but perhaps the most applicable were identified by STRATFOR as "relaxed awareness," "focused awareness," and "high alert."[4] These are the three stages that security-aware individuals should move in and out of anytime they are not in their home or office.

Upon leaving one's residence, or upon picking up the protected individual, all individuals should be in a relaxed state of awareness (also referred to as condition "yellow"). The goal is to be alert to potential threats, while maintaining a relaxed mental posture. This means being able to function while moving through the day, engaging in conversation, driving, having lunch, etc., but never tuning out the world moving around you. More important, this level of awareness allows one the ability to remain in this state for an extended period of time without suffering mental exhaustion. While in this state, should some person or possible situation be detected that warrants more attention, you mentally move into the next level, that of "focused awareness" (also referred to as condition "orange").

Focused awareness means that you concentrate on the anomaly in your environment without letting other things distract you. It could be that the two miscreants you have spotted up ahead are totally unaware of you, your team, your family, etc. Your focused attention to this possible threat allows for you to make a decision prior to being forced into a decision. Do you cross the street, step into a store, or continue on your path. All of this will be decided relatively quickly, depending upon whether it is a protective detail, an outing with the family, or by yourself. If it is determined not to be a threat, then you fall back into the mode of relaxed awareness and continue on about your day.

Focused awareness is the frame of mind in which a protective team should operate when conducting an operation. You are keenly aware of your surroundings, your team members' locations, your weapons, and your equipment. Your reflexes are ready to respond, thus decreasing the possibility of being surprised and thereby decreasing your response time. You are, in a sense, ready to bring the fight.

However, should you determine the two men in the previous example are a clear and present threat to you, your team, or family, then you will switch into the last phase, that of "high alert" (also referred to as "condition red"). This phase requires immediate action on your part. Engage the hostile, implement immediate evasive maneuvers, and retreat out of the area, whatever needs to be done to remove the threat, or remove oneself from the threat (depending upon your weaknesses and strengths at the time). At this level, the human body is under enormous physical strain from the dump of adrenaline and cannot last in this phase for long without becoming mentally drained and devoid of rational thought.

One caveat to these levels of awareness, in particular, is being "tuned out" in a residence. While inside of a person's residence is statistically one of the safest places from becoming a victim of an organized targeted attack, the use of a ruse has seen increased use with lethal results. In fact, it has been found that the ruse is most often employed at the targeted individual's residence.[5] The ruse takes advantage of the reduction in one's guard, or awareness level, in order to get close to the target. Another aspect of the ruse that can be difficult to see through is the characterization or scenario employed. Some of the documented ruses have included a mail carrier delivering mail, a police officer, a priest, a person selling flowers, deliverymen, even plumbers.

Case in point: On Friday, December 18, 1981, at approximately 6 p.m. in a quiet neighborhood of Verona, Italy, U.S. Army General James Dozier was kidnapped by members of the Italian terrorist organization, the Red Brigades. The attack occurred when two men operating under the ruse of being plumbers, arrived to repair a reported water leak that was dripping into the apartment below Gen. Dozier's sixth floor apartment. As Gen. Dozier, buying the reasoning, let the two men in, he was suddenly rushed by two more men that had been positioned unseen outside the doorway. Gen. Dozier was subdued, bound, gagged, and forced into a waiting truck. It was later reported that prior to the attack, a member of the Red Brigades had posed as an employee of the local utility company in order to conduct close target reconnaissance of the apartment area.[6]

127

The key to this is to spend the extra second or two before opening the door to determine who it is. Was a delivery expected? Is the postal carrier the regular person? Was a repair person requested? If it is a solicitor, send them away or perhaps put some sort of "no solicitors" sign on the door. Finally, when opening the door, only open it enough to deal with the issue. Place your foot against it to prevent it from easily being forced open. Look at the person and the immediate area. Ultimately, it is up to you to the make the decision on whether to open the door.

At the end of the day, it falls on the individual, either team member or potential target, to be alert to the surroundings and what information is available about them. Remember, our adversary only has to be lucky once.

ENDNOTES

1. *Excellent Cadavers, The Mafia and the Death of The First Italian Republic* by Alexander Stille, Vintage Books, New York, 1995.
2. *The Mission, The Men and Me: Lessons from a Former Delta Force Commander* by Pete Blaber, Berkeley Publishing Group, 2008, 165–167.
3. Fury as Terrorists Kill Envoy by David Graves, Paul Anast, and Ben Fenton, Telegraph.co.uk, June 9, 2000, www.telegraph.co.uk/news/worldnews/europe/greece/1341819/Fury-as-terrorists-kill-envoy.html.
4. A Primer on Situational Awareness by Scott Stewart, STRATFOR, June 10, 2010, www.stratfor.com/weekly/20100609.
5. McGovern, Glenn, *Targeted Violence: A Statistical and Tactical Analysis of Assassinations, Contract Killings and Kidnappings*, CRC Press, Boca Raton, FL, 2010.
6. *Encyclopedia of Terrorism* by Harvey W. Kushner, Sage Publications, Thousand Oaks, CA, 2003, 109.

8

Overt versus Covert Details

No enterprise is more likely to succeed than one concealed from the enemy until it is ripe for execution.

Niccolo Machiavelli
The Art of War (1521)

Large signature operations based on multiple layers of security are the standard for federal agencies tasked with protective functions, such as the Secret Service and State Department, and rightly so. The level of official they are responsible to protect and the potential political and economic fallout that could arise from a successful assassination mandates this type of operation. More to the point, these federal organizations have the resources, funding, and manpower to carry out this level of operation on a sustained basis. When coupled with state and local law enforcement resources, the level of protection provided is very formidable.

With the exception of perhaps only a few locales, these types of operations are rarely, if ever, carried out by a municipal or county law enforcement (hereafter referred to as local law enforcement) organization, beyond that of serving in a support function. As such, lacking these resources, local law enforcement has traditionally made use of more covert techniques to accomplish similar goals. These discreet protective details work very well as long as operational security measures are well established and maintained by the team. More importantly, it requires that the circle of those in the "need to know" remains tight.

The nature of covert or discreet protective details is the polar opposite of the large signature operations. It is characterized by the use of unmarked vehicles without marked escort, communication through coded traditional radio (hopefully encrypted), and/or some other means. It also has a much smaller signature in terms of the number of personnel and vehicles used, which thereby draws less attention. However, the true strength of the covert protective operation lays in its ability to blend in, to remain anonymous, and to prevent the adversary from knowing when, where, and how it is to be conducted.

If one thinks about what it means to be covert, themes such as military special operations, intelligence outfits, and even James Bond, perhaps comes to mind. This is understandable as most relate "covert" to being secret, just as it is defined in Webster's dictionary.[1] In protective operations and more specifically, covert protection, the terms *subterfuge* and *guile* should be added to the equation. What good is it if a protective team has taken all the necessary steps of running a quality covert detail, yet they always place the protectee in the same location, i.e., right side, rear passenger seat, second vehicle. Positioning the protectee in this manner is trained by state, federal, and corporate details, but more importantly, it is widely understood by the public at large. The simplistic reason for positioning the protectee in the rear seat is because that is where the vehicle approaches the curb to offload the dignitary or VIP (in the United States and many other countries). In law enforcement protective operations, a curbside offload fronting a building is a predictable and dangerous tactic.

If an organization is going to make the effort to run a protective operation in a covert manner in order to enhance overall security, then they must employ some subterfuge and guile, thereby avoiding a pattern. Unlike corporate details, when transporting a chief executive officer, or when a state or federal law enforcement organization transports a dignitary, law enforcement usually does not have to worry about the overall comfort or wishes of the protectee. This is primarily due to their providing protection because of evidence or intelligence that leads law enforcement to strongly believe that the person's life may be in grave danger. As a result, the protective detail is in charge and should have the flexibility to conduct the operation as it sees fit. This is a freedom that many protective details may not enjoy, but one that can make all the difference.

Unfortunately, as it becomes more widely known within an agency that a protective function exists, there are going to be times when the unit is tasked with providing protection for the agency leadership or similar persons. This is the nature of the beast, and absent any spikes in the threat assessment on that particular individual, the unit may be forced to assume a more "traditional" dignitary protection stance. Obviously, this can mean arriving in the front of locations, possibly in view of media and the public at large.

Given this compromise of the protective function for public events, an even more focused OPSEC (operational security) is required to ensure that weapons, personnel, and vehicle information is prevented from being revealed unnecessarily (as detailed in Chapter 7). One method to do this is to obtain a uniformed presence at the drop-off point. Short of this, it is strongly recommended that two or more detail members be pre-positioned near or within the crowd at the arrival point in an undercover role with at least one other in an overwatch position. This will limit the number of individuals linked to the vehicle and the team. As in all operations, it is important to keep a record of what tactics, techniques, and equipment were visible to the public, and thus considered compromised.

Historically, there have been many attacks in which—had the protective detail switched up their tactics—the tragic outcomes might have been vastly different. We will begin with perhaps one of the most often employed and certainly most easily recognizable indicators of the protective detail: the three-vehicle motorcade. Ideally, all three vehicles (sedans or sport utility vehicles) would have all four-passenger windows as well as the rear window darkly tinted. Vehicle such as these can draw attention, but that is not an immediate concern, the reason being that if a motorcade such as this is witnessed driving by, it will draw the attention of people not accustomed to such a thing and who will no doubt wonder the reason, but there is no loss of security. Once passed, it is quickly forgotten.

If the targeted victim and the protective detail are under hostile surveillance, then the adversary is already aware of the vehicle configuration, so there is no compromise. The key is that while not having the windows tinted may not draw the attention of a third party, it benefits the adversary as anyone can see inside and readily identify the exact location in which individuals are seated, i.e., the target. The tinted-windowed vehicles can draw more third-party awareness, but at the same time can prevent the adversary from obtaining easy target identification/location.

The benefit of employing three similarly configured vehicles with tinted windows allows for the protectee to be placed in one of nine different locations (i.e., the use of guile and subterfuge). If the protective detail employs good OPSEC, then they can and should move the protectee's position within the cars themselves as well as within the motorcade on a continuous basis. Now, there are those who will argue against switching up the protectee's location because in the event of an attack, in the heat of the moment, the team may lose valuable seconds trying to find the protectee.

Certainly, this is a possibility, but the likelihood for this to occur with a competently trained team is remote. While operational, the team will know in which vehicle the protectee is traveling. Even if unsure of the exact positioning within the vehicle, the time it would take to visually sweep the interior is negligible. Another problem some may have is the placement of the protectee in the front passenger seat. If the windows are tinted dark enough and the front visors of the vehicles are down, then it would be difficult for anyone to see inside and confirm the target's location.

An additional benefit of similarly configured vehicles is the ability to split up into three separate directions. Again, in order to be effective it requires solid OPSEC at the beginning. Additionally, when employing this tactic, each vehicle should be well armed with the same number of personnel aboard. Having one vehicle with three on board and the others with only a driver defeats the purpose of attempting to create illusion.

Remember that in practicing good OPSEC, if a team considers placement of the protectee in the front passenger seat, that cannot be the first and only time the front passenger visors are down as this would be a strong indicator of the target's positioning. Given the nature of undercover vehicles, and if equipped with Code 3 equipment (as discussed in Chapter 2), then if a visor red/blue light is set up, it could easily become SOP (standard operating procedure) that the visor is always down in all cars in case of the need to switch on the lights and siren.

Every tactic has its strengths and weaknesses. On covert details, the use of vehicles with darkly tinted windows allows for the positioning of the principal to be varied, which is certainly a strength, in that it makes the direct targeting more difficult for an adversary. On the flip side, using several tinted-windowed vehicles in succession will inherently attract some attention, lessoning the overall "covert" nature of the operation. However, if several vehicles are used, targeting of a specific individual will be delayed for at least a short period of time.

The goal here is to prevent the easy identification of a targeted victim's location within the motorcade. It is also to delay an adversary at the ambush site, long enough to buy the protective team some precious seconds to react. Perhaps more importantly, this tactic can cause an adversary to rule out certain attack plans altogether. A caveat to this is that under no circumstances should the protectee ever drive a vehicle.

Case in point: On Thursday, July 29, 1999, at approximately 9:15 a.m. in Colombo, Sri Lanka, Dr. Neelan Tiruchelvam was assassinated. The attack occurred as he sat in the left rear passenger seat, as was his routine, of his chauffeur-driven vehicle, stuck in traffic. A suicide bomber walked through the traffic and approached Tiruchelvam's car from behind, passing a vehicle with Tiruchelvam's protective detail positioned behind him, and upon reaching the left rear side and confirming his target, detonated the device. The blast killed the bomber and Tiruchelvam, injuring the chauffeur and the protective detail member positioned in the front seat of the vehicle.[2]

The switching up of the subject's position within the motorcade offers a considerable amount of mitigation against explosive-based attacks. Most improvised explosive devices (IEDs) and vehicle-borne improvised explosive devices (VBIEDs) used in assassinations have attacked a specific vehicle within a motorcade. This is primarily due to a motorcade using between one and three vehicles, or where the position of the protectee has remained constant. This is also due to the amount of explosive material used in these devices and their proximity to the targeted vehicle. While there have certainly been explosive attacks that have destroyed more than one vehicle in a motorcade, such as the attacks on Magistrate Giovanni Falcone on May 23, 1992, in Sicily, and Prime Minister Rafik Hariri on February 14, 2005, in Beirut, these are thankfully in the minority due to the tremendous amount of explosive material required.

For this subterfuge to work properly, however, requires the protected individual to be positioned in a vehicle and in a motorcade without being seen by potential hostile surveillance. When this is not possible, then the use of similar vehicles for the motorcades becomes worth its weight in gold. If it is believed that the protectee's position may have been compromised, at some point along the route the cars simply switch up their position. As long as all three cars are identical (short of license plates, which, if the fronts plates have been removed, are of minimal risk) and all three are practicing good OPSEC, then security should be tight. The problem comes when one person or one car makes a mistake.

Case in point: On the morning of Thursday, November 30, 1989, Alfred Herrhausen was assassinated by a technically advanced IED in Frankfurt, Germany. He was traveling to his office in a motorcade consisting of three armored Mercedes Benz 500SEs. At an intersection within 500 meters from his residence, terrorists, reportedly with the Red Army Faction, had cached a 20–30 kilo IED with an infrared beam-triggering mechanism. Herrhausen was traveling in a common location for VIPs, namely the second vehicle on right rear passenger seat. However, it was reported that he was a heavy smoker and as such, kept a window partly open to allow for the smoke to escape. As the lead vehicle passed, a terrorist positioned in the dense foliage along the side of the street turned on the device activating the infrared beam, which was projected across the width of the street. As Herrhausen's vehicle broke the beam, the device was triggered and detonated, launching a five-pound, eight-inch-diameter copper plate, killing him.[3]

When traveling in a covert, multiple-vehicle motorcade protective detail, it is important that the vehicle not separate unless it is deemed appropriate and not draw unnecessary attention. One potential problem that can commonly arise is when approaching signal-light-controlled intersections. The driver of the lead vehicle should not attempt to "make the light," as it is unlikely that the whole motorcade will get across (short of exigent circumstances, of course), thereby separating the individual cars. The lead driver should remain constantly aware of the following vehicles and the principal. Without the presence of immediate support and backup, the motorcade is strongest when together.

Prior to any motorcade detail, whether covert or not, all the drivers should drive the primary and secondary routes in all directions during the projected times of travel. This allows the drivers to obtain a familiarity with the areas they will be operating in and to note the potential problem areas, such as sharp, blind corners, tricky intersections, etc. The drivers can determine the authorized (i.e., legal) speeds as well as emergency speeds as the traffic and roadway permit. This can be especially important if a sharp corner or turn must be negotiated. In the United States, many of these areas have signage indicating the safe speed to travel at these points. In some cases, 15 mph means precisely that, 15 mph. However, in other cases, that 15 mph turn can easily be traveled at twice that speed or more if needed.

When traveling these routes in preparation for a protective motorcade, the drivers should drive vehicles that are not going to be used on a detail, but at the same time are of similar size and capability. This prevents unintended operational compromise while at the same time obtaining correct determination of roadway and vehicle limitations. Finally, the drivers can familiarize themselves with those locations identified as likely ambush points, thus allowing them to visualize potential scenarios and their avenues of escape.

One problem that can arise for a protective detail is when dealing with department heads who wish to drive their own vehicles. This can present an interesting dilemma for a detail, as the protectee will be driving. Obviously, whenever possible, all attempts to dissuade the person from this should be made. Similar events can occur when moving witnesses to new long-term locations. Whatever the reason, whenever possible, have a qualified individual drive the protectee's vehicle. There are other tactics for such situations, which for security reasons will not be discussed in this work.

More common when moving witnesses and victims out of an area where they reside., whether it is to be temporary or permanent, the individual needs access to a vehicle. Most likely, short of a rental car being arranged, the department will reach a decision for the protectee to take his/her own vehicle. If the protective team is lucky, the protectee's vehicle is parked in a location that is easily accessible. The keys are merely provided to an operator who goes out with the team and drives the vehicle away, preferably in the dead of night.

Unfortunately, Murphy's law often comes into play in these cases. If the vehicle is in the garage of a hostile party, it becomes trickier. Certainly, a warrant could be obtained, but on those occasions, it is best if protectees can take the vehicle with them when they leave. Whatever is ultimately the case, the key for a protective team is to ensure it is not followed. Some time also should be spent in removing all easily identifying marks, items, etc. (as detailed in Chapter 7), to prevent its being recognized by an adversary.

Another way of operating in a covert fashion is in disguising the protectee. At least one law enforcement agency in Northern California maintains a collection of clothing, hats, sunglasses, wigs, etc., for the purpose of hiding the identity of the protectee. While this may seem comical to some, and certainly there can be some friendly jokes while selecting the appropriate disguise, it is based on a solid theory. Intelligence agencies around the world have made use of disguise during their operations, including moving people out of hostile countries. If it works for them, it can certainly work for protective teams. If the adversary cannot determine who the target is, they cannot carry out the attack.

In law enforcement, those protected often have easily recognized tattoos that have to be covered. At the same time, modern technology has provided teams with the ability to add tattoos to those that do not normally have them. Wigs, shoes, even clothing can all serve to change the protectee's appearance. The goal, of course, is to change the person's appearance without appearing outrageous (i.e., the over-the-top baseball cap with attached wig). They must blend in with the team and the surroundings.

The process of being covert also extends to the team members themselves. Often referred to as operating in the "black," it means the operators dress to fit the situation and area of operations. As opposed to a man in fatigues, black boots, and body armor with sidearm and assault rifle, the covert protective operator is in a suit or casual clothing consistent with the surroundings. This does not mean they are any less ready for action, but it preserves OPSEC and reduces potential third-party awareness. If an adversary cannot differentiate between the team and a protectee, then the goal of the discreet detail is accomplished.

Finally, with covert operations the team must practice sound operational integrity. This means only those that need to know are aware of the specifics of the operation. This means arranging the pickup and drop-off points at areas protected from view of the general public. It is only by concealing as much as possible from the public and adversary that the detail gains an advantage.

ENDNOTES

1. *Webster's English Language Desk Reference*, Random House, Gramercy Books, New York, 1999.
2. Peace-Maker as Terrorist Target by V.S. Sambandan, *Frontline*, 16, 17, August 24–27, 1999, www.hinduonet.com/fline/fl1617/16170970.htm
3. Head of Top West German Bank is Killed in Bombing Terrorist by Ferdinand Protzman, December 1, 1989, *The New York Times*, *World*, www.nytimes.com/1989/12/01/World/head-of-top-west-german-bank-is-killed-in-bombing-by-terrorist.html

9

Surveillance Detection

The most effective weapon on any battlefield, whether it be in combat, business, or life, is your mind's ability to recognize patterns

Pete Blaber
former Delta Force commander

Around the world and throughout history, a wide range of individuals have employed surveillance. Police officers surveil drug dealers, intelligence agents surveil terrorists, criminals and terrorists surveil each other, their rivals, the authorities, and, of course, their next target. Kidnappers, stalkers, serial offenders, even jealous spouses, all surveil their victims. The point is the "watching" of another individual is used by a very diverse group of people and professions. Anyone targeting another individual, for whatever the reason, needs to employ some sort of surveillance for a period of time in order to obtain the information needed to conduct an attack. As such, those individuals aware of this fact will be more alert in order to detect its presence.

Case in point: In 1983, Italian authorities raided a safe house of the Red Brigades terrorist organization. Inside they recovered a manual, a portion of which dealt with the issue of surveillance of individuals.[1] Translated, it roughly stated, "If the hours of leaving work show too much irregularity, it is necessary to fix a surveillance of the car trip from the house to the office and continue throughout the day. The best time for kidnapping is at the end of a day when the man is tired and he's going home, but if the victim shows too much irregularity—he doesn't have a routine every day—start from the beginning of the morning when he leaves home and take him all through the day."

137

Just as a police officer prepares for the service of an arrest warrant on a specific individual, in targeted attacks the adversary will want to select the location for the ambush that offers the greatest chance of success. This therefore requires the adversary to conduct successive surveillance and reconnaissance operations of the target and the areas consisting of the work place, the residence, frequented areas, and all known routes in between. The reverse side of this coin is the more frequent the surveillance, the more chances there are of their being detected (especially if the frequent tracking occurs within a narrow period of time, such as a few days). Before delving into the mechanics of surveillance detection, it is important that first a common misconception is clarified. This is the difference between *countersurveillance* and *surveillance detection*, as they are more and more often used interchangeably, when they are in fact not the same.

Countersurveillance is a technique used mostly by intelligence operatives to exploit an adversary once the hostile presence has been detected; hence, surveillance detection is an aspect of countersurveillance. Countersurveillance is a proactive process that can range from the crude techniques commonly employed by street level drug dealers (which is really more akin to crude mobile surveillance detection) to highly sophisticated runs employed by professional intelligence officers that can last several hours. However, for this subtle art to be performed correctly and efficiently requires years of practice. In fact, according to Antonio J. Mendez in his book, *Master of Disguise: My Secret Life in the CIA* (William Morrow and Co., 1999), it was common, prior to their taking a post overseas, for agents to practice countersurveillance operations against upwards of 20 surveillants at a time, many using disguise and multiple vehicles. When countersurveillance is employed by seasoned practitioners, it is used to identify the vehicles and individuals conducting the surveillance, as well as their methodology. This information is then used by an individual to thwart the hostile surveillance.

Surveillance detection, however, is the "observation of people, places, vehicles, and locations" for the "purpose of determining whether or not surveillance is being conducted."[2] The key to this process is the TEDD acronym, standing for time, environment, distance, and demeanor. Individuals seen repeatedly over *time* in different *environments* over *distance* and/or who display an unusual *demeanor* provide an indication of the possible presence of hostile surveillance. One of surveillance detection's best attributes is that it is a relatively easy process to learn, and more important, it can and should be used by everyone who may be targeted.

Beyond the individual, surveillance detection can greatly enhance any protective unit and must play an active role in all operations.

For protective teams, the information needed to be collected by our adversary is known to us in law enforcement (think back to any time you have hunted down a wanted fugitive and the information you sought to accomplish the goal). Therefore, we know where our adversary will need to go in order to acquire it. This knowledge then provides a unit with the foresight and ability of detecting hostile surveillance at one or all of the four main attack locations: the home, office, frequented areas, and during routes of travel.

The methodology of surveillance detection focuses primarily on static and mobile surveillance. It should be considered an early warning system, which is very important, as a person can never know with any certainty when they are or maybe targeted for attack. Many people receive threats as part of the job without ever being attacked. There are also those that have been attacked as a result of their job without ever receiving a threat.[3] However, an important aspect to keep in mind is that if surveillance is ever detected, there is no way to determine at what stage in the attack planning process the adversary has reached (refer to Chapter 5 for more information). The detected surveillance operation could be early on, or it could very well be the day of the attack. Therefore, any suspicions of its potential presence need to be reported and dealt with immediately.

While it is conceivable for a hostile group to compartmentalize the operation resulting in the members of the hostile surveillance team being completely different from the group responsible for conducting the attack, it is of little consequence to the potential target. However, as reported by a "reformed" Mexican Sinaloa cartel hit man during an interview with Reuter's reporters in June, 2010, he and a team would wait at a safe house for the signal. The team had already viewed photos of the targeted individual and would wait for a phone call indicating the target's location. Once received, the team would travel to the area and carry out the operation.[4] This clearly demonstrates the separation of the intelligence collection and direct action functions in place by at least one of the cartels.

Generally speaking, however, most hostile organizations do not have enough trained or competent manpower, and even if they do, this is more of an issue for an investigating agency after the fact. However, no group with an ounce of professionalism is going to carry out an operation after only looking at photos, videos, and reading reports. Unless the hit is going to be some uncalculated drive-by spray-and-pray with automatic weapons (which obviously always has to be considered, but the background of an organization obtained as part of the assessment will provide the answers to this question), then at the very least, the leaders of the attack cell will most probably want to put some "eyes on target" prior to going operational.

> *Case in point*: On March 19, 2002, a Tuesday at approximately 2100 hours, Marco Biagi, a senior government aide was assassinated outside of his home in Bologna, Italy, by members of the Red Brigades. Prior to this death, he had received a number of threats, including one phone call in which the caller stated, "Now you're left without your angels."[5]
> This call provides clear indication that someone had been maintaining surveillance on Señor Biagi, a fact that was apparently ignored by the Italian government. While it is not known who exactly carried out this surveillance, what is clear is that someone had been watching Señor Biagi, and most likely for an extended period of time. In this instance, based on the context of the threat, the surveillance detection was provided by the adversary.

Situational awareness is a key component to surveillance detection. It can be defined as being observant of one's surroundings and identifying potential threats. As with surveillance detection, it can be easily learned and employed by anyone without a specific training regime. Part of developing one's situational awareness requires one not to become paranoid of danger at every corner, but to develop what has been referred to as a relaxed awareness. As has already been said, it is not possible for any individual to be constantly "switched on" 24 hours a day, seven days a week and, further, it is not healthy.

Even the best trained operatives in the world have times when they just fade out to their surroundings. This is why the statement from the Irish Republican Army after their attempt on the life of then-Prime Minister Margaret Thatcher on October 12, 1984, "We only have to be lucky once, you have to be lucky, always" is so apropos. The key is to be cognizant of your surroundings as you move through the day without being paranoid that an attack might be imminent. Remaining in the relaxed awareness state, the individual still looks for indicators of potential hostile activity, signs that they may be under surveillance or worse.

SURVEILLANCE BASICS

In order for an individual to conduct surveillance detection, it is important to have a firm understanding of the methods of surveillance. There are three levels of surveillance: mobile, static, and technical. Each has their own strengths and weaknesses for both the target and the adversary. Beginning with the static surveillance position, the ideal location will provide the surveillant with a good view of the target area. It will be a location that allows a surveillant to remain for an extended period of time without raising suspicions. It also must provide some method of documenting what is seen, but that again does not raise suspicions. With the advent of smart phones, net books, iPads, etc., all of which provide a method of documentation of activities observed, it would not be uncommon or suspicious to see these in use on a surveillance operation.

Recalling the cycle of attack as explained in Chapter 5, for surveillance detection to work, practitioners need to be aware of where in the cycle they are most apt to detect the hostiles. The two stages that have the best chance for detection are "target selection" and "operation planning." The reason is that these two phases require a person to put eyes on the target and thereby become susceptible to detection.

The keys to detection of static surveillance are time and demeanor. This means to watch the potential hostile surveillance points for signs of individuals using poor tradecraft. This requires some time training in watching people, but is a skill most cops have already acquired. Has the person touched their coffee in a while at the café? Should he have finished that newspaper on the park bench long ago? Has she let the last several buses pass while remaining at the bus stop, etc.? The bottom line is, have the people been acting consistent with what they seem to be doing or where they are located?

For those with surveillance experience, remember how difficult it was conducting it for the first time. The constant feeling you had been burned while in the position of the "eye" (which is the term associated with the individual with direct visual of the target). How difficult it seemed to act natural, and all of this after you had been trained in conducting surveillance. These same feelings affect the adversary, but perhaps to a worse degree as many if not most have had little to no training in conducting surveillance operations. The goal then is to watch for and identify the out of ordinary events and to then be able to correlate them with other observed activity until the hostile surveillance presence is confirmed.[6]

To perform mobile surveillance effectively takes more training, time, and personnel. Fortunately, for those of us in law enforcement and security, most criminals and many terrorists do not have the necessary skills or manpower to conduct mobile surveillance to the level of a government agency or private security corporation. For motorcades, it could be beneficial to select detection points (which will be discussed later in this chapter) that can occur via a mobile platform.

Mobile surveillance detection requires two things: time and distance. This means the more often a person and/or vehicle is seen over an extended period of time and distance, the more likely they are under surveillance. Given the general lack of numbers of personnel available to a criminal and/or terrorist organization, the more likely they will have to perform the surveillance using between only one to a few surveillants. Anyone who has spent any time conducting surveillance knows doing it alone is exceedingly difficult. It can only be done for a relative short distance (i.e., time and distance) without increasing the risk of exposure. In fact, perhaps only by the "step method" can it be performed covertly with little risk of detection. Should a hostile surveillance team employ the more advanced "step" surveillance, it is unlikely to be detected even by trained observers. The "step" surveillance methodology is an interesting technique in that it can be used by both the hostile surveillance against a target and vice versa with equal effect. However, for surveillance detection, it requires a much higher degree of familiarity with the area being traveled.

When employed by a hostile organization, the step surveillance process provides one of the more covert methods of identifying the route(s) of travel by a target, but is also the most time consuming. Further, given the amount of time the malefactor is required to be physically present around the target, the more chances there are for detection and/or compromise. The technique involves the hostile surveillants to follow their target for short distances before breaking off. For instance, beginning with the best known starting location, the office, the surveillants will follow the target for several blocks to a couple of miles depending on the nature of the route before breaking off. The next day, the surveillants will pick up the surveillance at the break-off point and again follow for a few blocks to a couple miles before breaking off again. The next day, the surveillance begins again at the last break-off point, and the process continues until the residence or frequented location and route of travel have been identified.

For this technique to work, however, requires the target to travel the same route and to travel around the same time. The dangers of taking the same route have already been covered in some detail in this work and countless others. Leaving locations at the same general times really empowers a hostile surveillance presence by allowing them to stage themselves at the last possible moment before the target is known to travel. The benefit is perhaps no more noticeable then when conducting the "step" surveillance technique as well as the attack itself. When the target departs a location at the same general time each day, the hostile surveillants can determine the amount of time to travel the distance and stage themselves at the pickup point right before the arrival of the target. This, of course, reduces the chance of detection by a third party. By changing up the times traveled, the adversary is forced to have an individual positioned at the starting point to advise the cohorts of the departure. Hence, the changing of the times of travel and routes of travel is the single easiest way of defeating or at the very least complicating the "step" process.

The "step" process also can be employed by a potential target in order to identify the presence of hostile surveillance and is similar, but reversed. In this method, the team or individual believing surveillance has been detected turns at an intersection while heading in the same general direction of travel. At the next intersection or a couple after, a turn is again made and so on. The goal is that with each turn, the likelihood that another person or vehicle is coincidentally traveling the same route is significantly reduced. However, any trained surveillance operators, especially in counter surveillance, will detect this maneuver immediately.

Mobile "foot" surveillance can be even more difficult, especially for those having little to no training. However, for the vast majority of attacks targeting an individual, this type of surveillance is not required. The exception to this would be for any targeted person making use of public transportation. It stands to reason that an adversary would want to tail an individual to determine what form of public transportation is taken and from what stop did the target ultimately exit. The issue of public transportation presents an interesting problem not only for protective operations in general, but, in particular, surveillance detection and situational awareness.

Case in point: On Wednesday, June 21, 1978, at approximately 8:30 a.m., in Genoa, Italy, the police commissioner for the town of Nervi, who was also the former Antiterrorist Squad chief, Antonio Esposito was assassinated by three members of the Red Brigades. He had boarded a bus as he did every day from his residence en route to his office. At the same stop location, a woman had also boarded and taken a seat near the bus driver. The bus continued along its route during which it made a number of stops, picking up additional passengers and dropping others off. At two separate stops, two men had boarded.

As Esposito continued to read his newspaper, one of the two men yelled out "Esposito" and fired his Nagant 7.65 caliber revolver striking Esposito in the chest and neck from a distance of approximately two feet. The second man, using a 9 mm pistol fired two rounds, striking Esposito in the abdomen and groin area. At this point, the passengers were screaming, the woman who had boarded originally with Esposito moved and was standing directly behind the driver. She yelled for the driver to stop the bus. When the bus came to a stop, the two men and the woman dashed out, but not before one of them fired two more rounds, striking Esposito again. They then fled in a car that was waiting at the nearby corner.[7]

This same scenario could easily have played out on a number of platforms beyond a bus, including subways, trains, local trolleys, etc. Surveillance detection in this environment can only be described as a nightmare. Due to the nature of public transportation, it would not be the least bit suspicious for a single individual to enter a subway/bus at the same stop and exit at same stop or continue on to the very next one and beyond. With the vast amount of human traffic entering and exiting at each stop along the route, a team of surveillants could easily maintain a watch on their target, similar to the "step" surveillance method previously discussed, with little to no chance of being discovered (referred to as being "burned").

To conduct surveillance detection in such a high pedestrian traffic environment will truly require a person to be completely "switched on" while on board. Considering the spectrum of individuals traveling, from business-suited professionals to kids to the homeless, identification becomes exceedingly difficult. However, hostile surveillance points (HSP) will most likely be located at those areas providing a complete view of the exits. The adversary in the HSP also will want to be near an exit to allow for a quick escape in the remote chance of detection. This should be kept in mind by any individual and/or team making use of public transportation.

The final method of surveillance is accomplished by technical means and includes the use of binoculars, cameras, audio and video recorders, etc., and is often used in conjunction with mobile and static surveillance. It also includes surveillance via global position satellite (GPS) tracking devices. While, these are primarily used by law enforcement and intelligence agencies, hostile organizations can acquire them, too. The prime benefit to these devices is that they allow the surveillants to stay out of sight for extended periods of time. The only risk of exposure is during the installation and recovery periods. Generally, the only way the device can be detected is via physical inspection of the vehicle, as you would if expecting an attack by booby-trap device. Even then, depending upon the expertise of the installer, the device may be nearly impossible to find short of a complete vehicle teardown.

Another less obvious potential method of surveillance that is becoming more and more common is via "remote" video surveillance. This equipment is readily available and can be surreptitiously installed at a location to monitor a residence (such as across the street, hidden in vegetation, unbeknownst to the neighbor). More importantly, it can be remotely accessed via the Internet. Some new technology applications with cell phones also allows for remote tracking of individuals that is meant as a means of social networking among friends. As with many new technologies, it could easily be used by a hostile party to track a potential target's movements.

THE SURVEILLANCE DETECTION
PROCESS (STATIC AND MOBILE)

Before surveillance detection can be effectively implemented, those tasked with the job must be familiar with the areas the detection is going to be performed. This requires site surveys of the residence, office, frequented areas, and general routes of travel into and out of these areas. It is particularly important in suburban residential area as the possible routes in and out tend to be highly constricted, leaving between one and perhaps up to four ways. Ideally, surveillance detection begins well before any protective operation. The adversary will begin the planning of the operation once the target has been determined, just as any police officer prepares for an arrest warrant service or a military unit prepares for an attack. The first step is surveillance and reconnaissance (S&R) of the target and the area.

If performed as suggested, before a threat situation arises, then those team members conducting the survey will be allowed greater freedom in completely examining the area both internally looking out and externally looking in. If, however, for whatever reason a baseline survey has not been conducted, then the surveyors need to be cautious and alert for the possible presence of hostile surveillance.

The first stage is to identify the areas at which an adversary is most likely to be positioned in order to surveil the target office, residence, or frequented location. Ideally, this should be considered from the perspectives of those highly trained in conducting surveillance as well as those with no experience (thereby obtaining the "amateur" factor). It is hoped that this will allow the team to obtain the perspectives of professionals as well as the inexperienced gangster/crook. Once these hostile surveillance points (HSPs) are identified, the surveyors move to the next stage. The team should then identify locations referred to as surveillance detection points (SDPs), in which they could set up to watch these hostile surveillance positions. In cases where advance set up is not possible, identification of those areas most likely to be utilized by hostile surveillants allows for detection teams to drive through an area and spot the potential hostiles prior to the arrival of the protectee.

For protective operations/details employing a surveillance detection functionality, the ideal situation is for the advance car to be able to sweep through ahead of the detail. While it theoretically could be accomplished by a single person driving, it is preferable to have a two-person car, containing either females or one of each sex. (Two males, especially hard-trained operators, can easily raise suspicions.) This works most effectively in residential areas, given the general lack of surveillance positions to blend in with. Obviously, if your targeted victim's home is across the street from a park or shopping center, such as detailed in Figure 9.1, things become more complicated.

Figure 9.1 Residences located across from commercial areas, such as these, present considerable problems for surveillance detection. The nature of the area provides a multitude of covers for action from a number of different locations and angles.

146

The old adage about poor planning and the resulting performance is exceptionally true here. The more detailed the survey, the more likely the team is to detect possible hostile surveillance and lessen the potential of false positives or "ghosts," as they are more commonly referred to in intelligence vernacular. Questions, such as, Who resides in the area? What cars are normally present and where are they parked (remember the general public are creatures of habit and, therefore, will park in the same general area every time they return)? What areas are viable positions to maintain an "eye" on the frontage of the location, targeted vehicle, etc.? What areas of potential HSPs are visible from the interior of the location?

While detailed in nature, it can be refined to the times the potential target is known or likely to be in the area, that is, morning and evenings about one hour before and after the normal arrival/departure times. This will help narrow down the amount of work, at least regarding cars and pedestrians that habitually move or are in the area. This, however, brings up the issue of a target's family. Statistically speaking, families are rarely targeted by hostile organizations, with the exception being groups that kidnap for ransom. If the spouse works and any children attend school, then most of the time, all will be leaving around the same general time frame.

Thus, the surveillance detection workup needs little to any modification. If the spouse does not work, then short of taking kids to school, there is generally a lack of any routine schedule of travel. This lack of routine reduces the likelihood of attacks as it forces surveillance to be present beyond normal departure/arrival times—hence, the general lack of attacks documented as occurring during the weekends.[8] The one caveat to this is if the potential target tends to transport the children to school. This should be considered a "frequented" location, and a surveillance detection survey must be completed. Interestingly, attacks staged near schools have generally occurred immediately after the targeted victim has dropped off the children.

Case in point: On Tuesday, December 8, 2009, at approximately 7 a.m. in Tegucigalpa, Honduras, Julian Aristides Gonzalez, the general director (and retired Honduran army general) of an organization tasked with combating drug trafficking, was assassinated. The attack occurred just after Director Aristides had dropped off his daughter at her school. Two men riding tandem on a motorcycle pulled up alongside and opened fire with an automatic weapon, killing him.[9]

147

As part of the detection workup, the potential hostile surveillance positions should include the routes into and out of an area. This route analysis can be focused to perhaps a block or two, depending upon the area and the amount of traffic flow during the identified times. Additionally, there should be an examination of all routes for areas that overlap, especially those that have to be traversed, regardless of what route is ultimately selected. The reasons for this are twofold. First, each time a target passes a street or intersection, he/she increase their route potential exponentially, even if they always travel the same streets. Secondly, the benefit to these "environmental" routines is that it allows for an adversary to stage farther away from a location, such as a home or office.

The greater the distance, the more difficult static surveillance detection becomes, given the increase in population and societal activity. If any portion of a route, but in particular an intersection, is identified as being one that a targeted individual has to traverse, a detailed analysis of said area absolutely needs to be undertaken, the reason being that the hostile surveillance realizes the dangers of detection that come with conducting surveillance within a constricted area. So, instead of positioning near a residence, they could set up around the identified intersection, thereby reducing the chances of detection. At the very least, that provides the adversary one more layer of security and ultimately a potential ambush point. Conversely, it adds to a protective team's work and creates a potential ambush point.

Case in point: On Thursday, September 4, 1969, the U.S. ambassador to Brazil, Charles Burke Elbrick, was kidnapped by members of the MR-8 Marist rebel group. Hostile surveillance of the target had determined that Elbrick, or perhaps more correctly, his chauffeur, was a creature of habit and traveled the same route each morning between the official residence and the embassy. On the morning of the attack, a female positioned herself up the street in a vehicle, but within sight of the rest of her six-person team. On spotting Elbrick's limo, she signaled her team, and as it passed by her, she pulled in behind. The limo slowed and completed a turn at an intersection at which point a car with five aboard pulled out in an intercept, preventing it from moving forward. The female lookout then blocked the rearward escape with her vehicle. The rebels jumped out armed, and Elbrick was kidnapped and ultimately held for four days.[10]

An additional issue that needs to be examined during the survey is that of parking locations. Whether the home or office, it is a common habit of most people to park in the same parking stall and/or general location.

(Ever attend a training course and switch your seat on the second and third day and see the look of confusion from the person who sat there the day before?) Hence, the importance of identifying the cars normally parked, type, and location near the residence of a potential target prior to the existence of any threats.

When selecting the surveillance detection points, one of the difficult factors is picking locations that have good cover and concealment. By "cover," it is meant the "operational cover," that is, your reason for being in the area. Your "cover for action," as this is known, must be convincing. This becomes increasingly more difficult the farther the surveillance detection operation gets out of areas of heavy public traffic and closer to residential areas (Figure 9.2).

Conversely, while heavy public areas provide good concealment for a surveillance detection team, it can be more difficult to detect the presence of hostile surveillance even when the HSPs have been identified. In

Figure 9.2 Areas combining residential and commercial areas are common in other parts of the world and increasingly in the United States. As depicted in the photo, it can be difficult to impossible to simply look and immediately spot the hostile surveillance operative. Only through time and distance and analysis can there be any real chance of detection.

residential areas, it is the adversary that has a more difficult time blending in. For surveillance detection teams in these areas, consideration of the surroundings is a must. The use of a onetime vehicle drive-by (in a non-cop-looking vehicle) with a man and a woman or two women on board (which can reduce suspicions) can be an effective surveillance detection platform. The jogger out for a run, a person walking a dog, etc., are effective surveillance detection ruses. These fit the area and allow for all of the HSPs to be checked. The use of a body wire on these operatives allow for the discreet broadcast of license plates, descriptions of vehicles, and people in the area.

Surveillance detection routes (SDRs) are a method of drawing out possible mobile surveillants. Unlike professional intelligence officers who, due to the nature of their work, employ very subtle SDRs, potential targets of violent attack have no need for subtlety. This, therefore, allows potential targets and protective teams to be more aggressive in their efforts to detect a hostile presence. After all, if hostile surveillance deems a potential target too difficult, the chances are they may select another target, which is documented as having occurred. While obviously far from ideal, it achieves the goal of preventing an attack on that specific individual. However, part of the goal of surveillance detection is identification of the subject in order to confirm if hostile. If hostile parties realize they may have been detected, they may break off the surveillance. However, there is no guarantee they will not be back, this time using better operational security (OPSEC) to prevent you from detecting them.

Ideally, the individual or protective team will have several SDRs available to them, spaced out over the range of their route. While the use of an SDR is not really needed or practical for one-time runs that are short in distance and duration, they should be incorporated for frequented routes of travel between the residence, the office, and the like. The benefit of this technique is that should anyone detect that anomaly, that violation of the TEDD principle, then an SDR can be run in an effort to confirm the hostile presence.

One of the easiest and perhaps most effective methods of a SDR that can be easily incorporated into one's daily activity is referred to as "channeling." This method dictates traveling on a long, straight roadway that has several possibilities for changing direction at the end. By traveling these "corridors," it forces surveillants to follow, thereby allowing for more of them to be more easily identified. Whenever possible, only those corridors should be selected that do not allow for a surveillant to run parallel, thus defeating the SDR. Using the Internet mapping systems will allow one to identify possible SDRs along routes of travel. However, all should be driven to confirm their viability.

BEHAVIOR PATTERNS

The adversary, in order to develop the target's behavior pattern, will next put "eyes on target" for some duration. This is perhaps the first point of vulnerability for the adversary. Just as cops worry about being "burned" on surveillance, so too does the adversary, and the actions taken can be identified by a trained observer. It, therefore, is important for any protective team assigned the surveillance detection function to understand the behavior patterns of the person to be protected in order to determine where they could become vulnerable to attack (this pattern analysis will also be important later in developing personal protection plans, as detailed in Chapter 10).

There are three patterns that drive a person's behavior and to a certain extent, a protective team. The first of the three is the *organizational* pattern, which is primarily activity driven by the target's profession. It could be as simple as having to travel to and from work each day. It would also include meetings required to attend, classes to be taught, etc.

The second of the three is the *operational* pattern, which is the activity surrounding how the target goes about their personal and workplace business. This could include using protective details, carrying a concealed weapon, changing up one routes of travel, even the number and type of vehicles used in a protective operation. It also could include how the person moves between locations during the work day.

The last of the three is the *personal* pattern, which as the name indicates, is the target's activity surrounding his or her family relationships, such as taking the kids to school (a pattern that has been exploited in several targeted attacks in the past), but could also include extramarital affairs and the activity surrounding them. It can be as simple as the evening walk with one's spouse. Once these are recognized, the adversary can begin to adapt to them.[11]

RUNNING THE SURVEILLANCE DETECTION OPERATION

Employing a surveillance detection operation or methodology provides an opportunity for the adversaries to show themselves. It can serve to confirm the threat as well as provide means of identifying the involved parties should they make an appearance. This also goes back to the topic discussed in risk management on identifying those in your organization most apt to be targeted. If the initial background and research is performed correctly, then the team already has the baseline surveillance detection work in their hands. All the team needs to do is refer to the plan prior to going out and setting up.

In preparing the surveillance detection, use of a chart or matrix is extremely beneficial in identifying the hostile surveillance positions and potential ruse cover, and the view each offers the adversary. With the "Keep It Simple, Stupid" (KISS) methodology, one of the better matrices is shown in Figure 9.3.

The matrix would, then, continue on to identifying each HSP possibility, a potential cover, and, most importantly, the view the position provides. One potential addition to the matrix for consideration would be the duration of time the cover would remain viable. Using the example of the coffee drinker at the café, the duration would be about one hour maximum. However, add a second person, a couple of women just chatting, or someone with a laptop and perhaps it could be pushed out to two or more hours before it might begin getting suspicious.

The same process holds true for the identification of the surveillance detection positions (Figure 9.4).

Making contact with subjects in hostile surveillance points, short of exigent circumstances, is strongly discouraged. Members of a surveillance detection or protective team should not break cover. Ideally, if the agency conducting the operation also controls the jurisdiction, then a marked unit could be sent as though someone called in a suspicious person.

Hostile Surveillance Points

HSP #	Location:	Cover	View	Duration
1	Cafe	Drinking coffee	Front entrance	1 h
2	Book store	Shopping/reading	Front entrance	1–2 h
3	Park bench	Reading/eating	Oblique view of front	1–2 h

Figure 9.3 The above matrix is a simple yet effective method of identifying the various hostile surveillance positions around a potential location, be it residence, office, or frequented location.

Surveillance Detection Points

SDP #	Location	Cover	View	Duration
1	Bus stop	Waiting for bus	HSP #1	30 min
2	Library	Reading	HSP #2	1–2 h
3	Street	Walking dog	HSP #1–3	1 h

Figure 9.4 As with the hostile surveillance position matrix, a similar method should be used to identify those locations where surveillance detection positions could be established.

Once the various points have been identified, the surveillance detection team needs to man the positions. As with any type of surveillance operation, it can get monotonous. Operators need to practice excellent OPSEC and stay within the operational cover the surveillance detection point demands. All information than must be routed to a command post or noted for later analysis.

ANALYTICAL FUNCTION

The absolute critical component to any surveillance detection operation is the analytical function. In fact, without it, it is very likely that potential hostile surveillance signs/signals will be missed. Similar people and vehicles seen around the office and the residence while traveling at frequented locations are all strong indicators that a hostile surveillance operation is underway. However, if no one is keeping track of this information, how will a team know? Only through data entry and analysis of the notes from operatives will anyone become aware that a suspicious vehicle noted at the office in the morning was seen around the residence in the evening.

There is an abundance of software available to an analyst, such as link analysis programs like i2™ Analyst Notebook, Quantum Secure, and SV3. Each has their strengths and weakness and some can be quite expensive. However, lacking access to these systems, an analyst could also use a spreadsheet program such as Excel® to track the events. It would then only require sorting the information to locate the commonalities. While not ideal, it is far better than not keeping track of any of the information generated.

SURVEILLANCE DETECTION COMBINED WITH PROTECTION

A common law enforcement response to a threat situation is to "park" a police vehicle in front of the targeted victim's home. This can be detrimental early on in a case if the threat has yet to be confirmed. If an adversary drives by and sees the police presence, he will most likely assume he has probably been burned. Depending upon an adversary's level of sophistication, he could do a number of things. He could decide to call it off, believing the cops are on to him. He may decide to strike at another location, or come in via a different route (i.e., through a backyard). Or worse for the target, the assassin may just lay low and wait for the heat to cool off and for law enforcement to discontinue their protection (see more on this in Chapter 10). He may even decide to engage the police officer prior to the targeted individual.

> *Case in point:* On Wednesday, June 17, 2009, at a little after 6 a.m. in Athens, Greece, Nektarios Savyas, a police officer and member of an antiterrorist squad, was shot and killed by four gunmen. He had been assigned a shift parked in front of the home of a woman in the witness protection program. He was sitting in his car, when four hooded gunmen approached and opened fire with more than 20 rounds killing Officer Nektarios.[12] The witness was, interesting enough, not harmed.

If the threat is deemed credible enough to position a police vehicle in front of a residence on a 24-hour, seven-day a week basis, then the protective operation needs to be ramped up. Ideally, the individual should be moved to a safe house (see Chapter 6) as it can provide the best security while being the least manpower intensive. If, for whatever reason, the safe house is not an option, and the targeted individual is to remain in place under 24/7 guard, then the detail on the static location should have at least three individuals, one positioned inside and the other two on foot on the grounds.

This setup provides adequate protection and will allow for the team to have breaks. By not being "parked" out front, but mobile on foot, those operators can stay in the shadows and monitor for potential hostile action/surveillance. For operational security, shift changes should not occur during normal arrival/departure times when hostile surveillance is most apt to be present.

PASSIVE SURVEILLANCE DETECTION

A disclaimer: What follows is strictly theoretical, the idea I had to deal with a widespread problem, but I was never able to employ. Several years ago a colleague of mine working for an internationally recognized high-tech firm, mentioned that the equally well known CEO did not have a protective detail. Further, this CEO was known to often walk in the downtown area for morning coffee, all while unattended. During subsequent research into targeted violence against corporate executives, I discovered that many did not have full-time protective details, if any at all. Even more amazing was the continued lack of protection for those CEOs who had suffered a kidnapping. Interestingly, it was often the CEO's decision to discontinue any protection due to the inconvenience.

Understandably, having a protective detail at all times could be enormously expensive as well as an imposition upon the CEO. However, the fact remains that some of these individuals are targeted for kidnap for ransom.

Case in point: On Tuesday, May 26, 1992, at approximately 8:55 a.m. in Mountain View, California, cofounder and then-president of Adobe Systems, Charles Geschke, was kidnapped. Geschke had just arrived to his office when a man approached using a ruse of being lost, allowing the initial distance to be closed without rising suspicion. As the two met, the man pulled a gun and grabbed Geschke, forcing him into a waiting car. Geschke was bound, blindfolded, and driven to a town some 60 miles away where he was held for five days before being rescued. After the attack, Geschke hired a protective service, but terminated the contract approximately a week later, stating they were too intrusive.[13]

While there isn't one answer that will work for everyone, when I started thinking about the problem and thinking about the cycle of attack, I pondered if a passive surveillance detection program might be the answer. The initial cost would come from the initial workup of the surveillance detection plan, site surveys, identification of potential hostile surveillance points, route surveys, identification of people, and, more importantly, the vehicles normally parked in the area around the residence and frequented locations (i.e., schools, churches, and gyms). Periodic surveillance of the "principal," both static and mobile, during the normal arrival/departure times would hopefully allow for the detection of any hostile presence.

While obviously not the ideal, it is perhaps a good compromise between having a full-/part-time protective detail and nothing at all. While it certainly wouldn't reveal or protect against the chance encounters, it might identify or deter the targeted attacks. It also would keep the costs in terms of manpower to a minimum, as it would only require between one and two individuals to check on a random schedule, and only for an hour or two at each time.

155

One other tool that would greatly enhance the ability of this passive surveillance detection/protection plan would be through the use of closed circuit television (CCTV). CCTV has become more and more commonplace in modern society. As a result, humans have become conditioned to their presence to the point that they often no longer take conscious notice. Certainly, those individuals targeting a potential victim will take note, but they will be forced to act in an unsuspicious manner when conducting surveillance and reconnaissance. This then prevents these individuals from spending too much time at a specific location so as to not bring unwanted attention to themselves. It also "generally" requires repeat visits to the same location over a period of time in order to collect the desired information. It works to a protective unit's benefit as the more the time and distance increases, the more often an unknown individual is seen at different locations and the more indications there are of a hostile presence.

As seen in the February 2010 assassination by an alleged nation/state hit team in Dubai, CCTV cameras present a considerable obstacle to the adversary and a wealth of information to the protectors. With modern technology, it is now possible to install a CCTV security system at a person's residence and have it monitored at another location via the Internet. While some may find even this too "intrusive," if it is pitched correctly, it would go a long way to enhancing the security footprint. The key is that the cameras would be positioned on a home's frontage, so that the previously identified hostile surveillance points could be monitored. This would mean the principal's privacy would be maintained for the most part, while enabling a security unit back at the office to monitor the area, as they would be doing anyway with the corporate security CCTVs.

TRAINING FOR SURVEILLANCE DETECTION

To truly understand the intricacies of surveillance detection, you have to perform it and train in it. Ideally, anyone assigned to protective operations will have some experience in conducting surveillance on suspects. This allows the operator to gain/have an understanding of the issues and nuances of setting up, maintaining an eye on the target, being discrete, and dealing with the intense boredom that it brings.

Practical training in surveillance detection is relatively easy to accomplish for a team and is, as with most tactical operations, the best way to learn how to perform correctly. Once an overview of the process is provided to a team, they should be sent out to scout a location. It does not have to even be related to the company. It could be a café, a volunteer employee's residence, a hotel, etc. In fact, a couple different areas would be preferable so that a team really develops the ability to identify a location's strengths and weaknesses from the perspectives of both the protective unit and the adversary.

Once the plans are worked up, the next stage is to run a "hostile surveillance" upon the location. It is a good idea to apprise the local police department of the training prior to running it in order to prevent any issues from arising; however, if the adversary and the SD team is performing their functions correctly, they shouldn't be identified. A good source of "bad guys" role players include spouses of the security unit, if unknown to others, retirees, current or former cops the unit might have connection with, etc. Once the team has run a few of these training operations and has the theory and process down pat, all that would be required is a periodic test or "red teaming" (see more in Chapter 5) of the surveillance detection plan.

It is the nature of organized targeted violence that the first time a person is aware he is a target is while he is being ambushed. This lack of foreknowledge of a pending attack mandates that government officials, journalists, activists, and anyone that could potentially be targeted for violence practice surveillance detection. The methodology is simple; the difficulty lies in the habitual implementation. For a protective team, there can be no excuse for not employing such a functionality.

ENDNOTES

1. *Combating Kidnapping and Terrorism in the Contemporary Operational Environment*, U.S. Army TRADOC G2 Handbook, No. 1.06, Ft. Leavenworth, KS, September 15, 2006.
2. *Surveillance Detection: The Art of Prevention*, by Laura Clark and William E. Algaier, Author House, IN, 2005 (3), 180.
3. *Targeted Violence: A Statistical and Tactical Analysis of Assassinations, Contract Killings and Kidnappings* by Glenn McGovern, CRC Press, Boca Raton, FL, 2010, 305.
4. I Killed, Cut off Heads: Says Repentant Mexico Hitman by Robin Emmott and Julian Cardona, Reuters Newswire, 6/18/2010, www.reuters.com/article/idUSNI8113865.
5. Red Brigades Admit Killing, *BBC News*, Thursday, March 21, 2002, http://news.bbc.co.uk/2/hi/europe/1885002.stm.

6. *Out of the Ordinary: Finding Hidden Threats by Analyzing Unusual Behavior* by John Hollywood, Diane Snyder, Kenneth McKay and John Boon, RAND Corporation, 2004, Santa Monica, CA, 155.
7. A Survey of Terrorism of the Left in Italy: 1970–78 by Vittorfranco S. Pisano, *Studies in Conflict and Terrorism*, 2, 3, 1979, 171–212.
8. *Targeted Violence*, McGovern, CRC Press, 2010, 305.
9. Honduras Anti-Drug Chief Shot Dead by Gunmen, Tuesday, December 8, 2009, http://news.bbc.co.uk/2/hi/8402521.stm.
10. Ex-Student Radical Might Become Rio's Next Mayor by Alexei Barrionuevo, *New York Times*, Sunday, October 26, 2008, www.nytimes.com/2008/10/26/world/americas/26iht-brazil.1.17247250.html?pagewanted=all.
11. First described by Pete Blaber in his book *The Mission, The Men, and Me: Lessons from a Delta Force Commander* (Berkeley Publishing Group, 2008) regarding his and his team's first studies into tracking down and capturing Osama bin Laden, 73–74.
12. Greek Terrorists Shoot Officer Guarding Witness, Thursday, June 18, 2009, *The Independent*, http://www.independent.co.uk/news/world/europe/greek-terrorists-shoot-officer-guarding-witness-1707915.html.
13. FBI Rescues a Kidnapped Businessman, June 1, 1992, *The New York Times*, http://www.nytimes.com/1992/06/01/us/fbi-rescues-a-kidnapped-businessman.html.

10

Levels of Protection and the Cessation of Protection

> In a free and open society, we simply cannot protect every person against every risk at every moment in every place. There is no perfect security ... in order to protect our country and defend our freedoms; we must continue to focus our resources on the areas that pose the greatest risk.

> **Michael Chertoff (February 14, 2006)**
> *U.S. Secretary of Homeland Security*

On Monday, July 19, 2010, at around 5:20 a.m. in Athens, Greece, there was a knock on the door at the home of Sokratis Giolias, a well-known local journalist. Despite the early hour, Giolias opened the door after three men in uniform informed him that his car had been stolen. As the door opened, the three men armed with 9 mm pistols opened fire with a volley of 16 rounds, 13 of which found their mark. As Giolias fell to the ground, the three assassins fled the scene in a nearby car. The car, which was found to have been stolen prior to the attack, was recovered later in the day, burned out.[1]

Giolias was the first journalist to be assassinated in Greece in over 20 years. The bullet casings matched those used in the killing of a police officer, as well as one found on the grave stone of a 15-year-old boy who was killed in 2008 by police. The attack was claimed by a group calling themselves the Revolutionary Sect, although there are many who question that admission. It was later reported that Giolias had refused to hire any protection, even though he admitted to having made many enemies.

With every threat/risk assessment, ultimately a decision has to be made as to the level of protection that is to be provided, if any. Without known or potential threats identified, the minimum level of protection is to educate individuals in providing for their own security (in the author's opinion, this should be the minimum that is provided to any threatened person even if deemed to be false). It is here where the divergence of the commonalities between federal protective agencies and local law enforcement are perhaps the greatest. With leaders of countries and high-ranking government officials, protection is a 24/7, 365 days a year operation. It therefore is known, planned, funded, and staffed. These large operations can also be provided by some state and larger local agencies providing details for governors and/or mayors; however, this is not often the case. Interestingly, it has been reported that as late as 1967, the then-governor of California, Ronald Reagan, did not have a full-time protective detail. Even today, many lawmakers do not have physical protection provided on a daily basis.

The decision on what level of protection to provide is wrought with unknowns. A decision should, of course, rely on the role of the principal, the nature of the case, the duration of the operation (i.e., trial, etc.), the adversary, and manpower and economic constraints. Couple this with the known or perceived threat, it is a decision that is not and should not be quickly made. It also is imperative to understand that this decision alone has the most potential for second-guessing and civil liability than perhaps all others, except the use of deadly force. Ultimately, when the perceived threat is gone, or perhaps worse, cannot be confirmed, what then?

Case in Point: On Wednesday, June 30, 2010, at approximately 9:30 p.m. in Ciudad Juarez, in the Mexican state of Chihuahua, Sandra Ivonne Salas Garcia, an assistant attorney general, was assassinated by members of the armed wing of the Juarez drug cartel, known as La Linea. The attack occurred as she was in transit between her office and her residence. Unknown to her, cartel gunmen were positioned in four vehicles, two parked in the parking lot of the nearby supermarket, a third was parked across the street near a park, and the fourth was in a parking lot of a restaurant.

In the attack on Salas, she was in the company of a two-member protective detail. At some point, either her or one of her two protective members became aware of the vehicles and increased the speed. As her vehicle neared a bridge, the cartel vehicles caught up and open fired with their weapons, killing Prosecutor Salas and one of her protective detail members, Omar Contreras. The second was injured but was picked up by an unknown vehicle shortly after the attack.

On July 5, 2010, one of the La Linea hitmen or *sicario* who took part in the attack was arrested and detailed the attack. He indicated they received information from inside the Attorney General's Office regarding her normal movements, which allowed them to be in the area of her office prior to her departure. He received a phone call advising of the hit the same day it occurred, and was told she had to be killed due to her investigating people detained at the Cereso prison.[2]

A *physical detail* is the most commonly thought of method for protecting an individual. If the decision is made to provide a physical detail, than a determination must be reached as to its makeup and its duration. Obviously, a considerable portion of this decision will be based on a threat assessment of some sort. While the single-person detail is widely used, this is the absolute least desirable and can often place the protector in as much risk as the protectee. Generally speaking, the minimum should be two individuals, one of which is the same sex as the protectee. This allows for at least one protective member around the principal at all times. This is even more of a requirement if the detail is scheduled to last the better part of the day as even protective operators will need to attend to personal needs at some point in the day.

A major factor in determining the type of protection operation to be mounted is the total length of time the protection is to be provided. For most agencies a 24/7 detail with a large team is exceedingly labor and resource taxing. Hence, the generally limited amount of time such an operation can be mounted, even with larger agencies. The question then becomes what type of protection is to be provided within an identified time period that achieves the goal while at the same time is sustainable? At the initial stage, is it to be 8 hours a day or on a 24-hour basis? Is it going to be just during the work week or seven days a week? Is it only during travel times from the house and office and vice versa? Does it require protection for family members? Of course, the number of protective members to be employed will have a direct impact on the hours used. As with the number of protectors, the duration of the day would be in direct relation to the threat/risk assessment. It also should be remembered that a good majority of attacks occur at or within close proximity to the victim's residence.

There is no one correct answer to this dilemma. First and foremost, it will depend upon the nature of the threat, followed closely in priority by the available resources of the responsible agency. A threat, in this instance, means identification of the adversaries, what are their history, attack methodology, and motivation for carrying out the threat?

- Are they known or believed to have killed witnesses and informants in the past?
- Are they known or believed to have attacked law enforcement or security officials in the past?
- Have they ever attacked a protective detail?
- Do they have a known or perceived high level of sophistication?
- Are automatic weapons and/or explosives known or believed to be in their inventory?

For each "yes" answer to these questions, the amount of protection provided needs to be increased concurrently. Understandably, organizations tend to err on the side of caution at least initially, providing a large protective signature. The problem with this is that an agency that is involved in providing this service can develop habits or a pattern of response. As previously discussed, a 24/7 multimember protective detail is extremely taxing to an agency's resources. If an agency habitually provides this service upon initial receipt of a threat only to scale it back week by week, then all a patient and observant adversary needs to do is wait until the situation favors his or her goal.

By way of example, several years ago I received an urgent telephone call from my then chief about members of a notorious prison gang targeting a prosecutor. The information was initially vague, but an informant had indicated that hostile physical surveillance had been conducted on the residence of the prosecutor. Obviously, things ramped up at a considerable pace; interviews were conducted to further refine the initial information. However, rather than allow for us to tighten the focus on who it was exactly that was being targeted, the picture became much more clouded.

In the end, the threat information consisted of the following:

The target was a white male.

The target drove a gold Cadillac.

The target lived in a house with a lot of roses planted in the front yard and had a wife and daughter who drove a large white SUV-type vehicle.

The target had recently been married, as evidenced by a photograph of the couple the informant claimed he had been shown.

The informant stated he had been sitting in a car near the house of the target and had seen the wife and daughter arrive home in a white SUV. He was not able to describe the target beyond that he drove a gold-colored Cadillac. The problem with the threat information was that the Cadillac and the home with the rose garden in front matched a particular prosecutor; however, when the informant showed us where he had taken part in the surveillance, it was in an area on the opposite side of town. The informant admitted he was high on methamphetamine during the surveillance to help pass the time (interesting proof of how boring static surveillance can be). Another problem was that the prosecutor who drove the Cadillac and lived at a house with a rose garden out front did not have a daughter, was not recently married and, further, was not and had never been involved in cases dealing with gangs, narcotics, and/or homicide.

However, in the residential area in which the surveillance and reconnaissance had allegedly taken place lived several prosecutors and investigators involved in gang prosecutions. The description of the photograph of the newlyweds was the most perplexing. That was until the then-head of the gang unit mentioned having a photograph on his desk, which matched almost identically what the informant had described.

This second bit of information caused considerable concern. How did the prison gang informant see the described photo? Was the photograph the same or just a coincidence? Was our office penetrated by the gang? (It certainly would not be the first time that a law enforcement office had been compromised by a hostile organization, but the implications of this were more far reaching.) Equally important, who was the actual target of this prison gang and how close were they to carrying out the hit? In the end, it was never confirmed. The informant provided just enough information for us to believe something hostile had occurred. However, the exact intent of activity, intent of the threat, and who was the actual intended target could not be determined (through the cloud of a methamphetamine-influenced surveillant).

Therefore, while steps were taken, eventually a decision had to be made. Do we provide protection to the two prosecutors that match the vague information? What form should that protection take: 24/7 physical security or just while at work, or do we just provide a concealed weapon and some training? What about the prosecutors living in the area of the hostile surveillance that were most likely to be linked to the gang in some fashion? Ultimately, there was no one correct answer. Such a decision needs to be made after a careful review of all of the known facts. I would add that in those situations where the "parent" hostile organization is known, experts on that organization should be taken into "the fold" to assist in making a determination as to the most appropriate level of protection.

Let us use the following scenario as an example of the decision-making process. A recently arrested inmate at the local county jail is heard over the jail phone indicating he wanted the prosecutor of the case killed. This information is passed to the prosecutor's office, which begins to rev up the "panic alarm." The law enforcement agency tasked with protecting the prosecutor's office, not wanting to look as though they are not taking it serious, quickly assigns a multiperson protective detail to the threatened prosecutor. This includes a motorcade of some configuration to and from work as well as an officer "parked" out in front of the residence during the hours of darkness. This continues for several days until the threat is finally analyzed. Was this response wrong? Not necessarily, as it still accomplished the mission of providing protection to the prosecutor. It did, however use up valuable resources and provided a potential adversary some insight into the agencies' methods of operation (if they were watching).

Perhaps a more efficient way to have handled it is as follows: First, with both the suspect and potential victim separated and their present locations known, the adversary in custody and the threatened prosecutor working in the office, there is no danger. Advising the prosecutor to remain in the office keeps him inside a secure location without the expenditure of any additional resources. Should the prosecutor need to appear in court, either a continuance could be obtained, another prosecutor could cover, or if need be, two officers could escort the prosecutor to court and back. Either way, minimal resource impact occurs, while providing time for other aspects of protective operations to proceed.

In the interim, the nature of the threat and risk analysis are run down and confirmed—if possible at such an early stage. While these cases do require some sense of urgency, they do not demand an immediate full law enforcement response. What was said in the threat? Was it a crook just venting about wanting to kill the prosecutor without any "real" intention of carrying it out? As part of this assessment, the analysts should try and determine at what stage in the attack cycle the adversary may be. If this threat is deemed to be legitimate, but the call was the initial instigation or "order," then there is some breathing room. This is due primarily to the attack cycle itself. Short of there being any familial or personal link between the prosecutor and the adversary (thus making identification and determining residence location infinitely easier), the individuals tasked with carrying out the operation will need time to plan out the hit.

Conceivably, if the law enforcement agency "went in heavy" immediately in the first couple of days, then continued to reduce the level of protection until it was ultimately canceled, all the work performed might be in vain, as the adversary had not even confirmed the identity, much less identified the location of the target. Hence, it is the author's opinion that instead of a "knee-jerk" response, the threat analyst should take a moment and look at the totality of what is known at the initial point the threat is received and the current location of the potential target.

Additionally, and this depends considerably upon the level of sophistication of the adversary, some thought should be given to possible misinformation. In the years following the September 11 terrorist attacks, there has been a plethora of warnings to law enforcement and corporate America of the possibility of false alarms. The theory being that a hostile terrorist organization would call in a bomb threat, leave a suspicious package, or park a car near a potential target in order to gauge the response. Conceivably, a hostile adversary targeting a specific individual could replicate this by providing an "anonymous tip."

If patient and done over an extended period of time, an adversary could gain a significant amount of intelligence information on how an organization responds to threats. Should this be suspected as having occurred, it indicates a much more dangerous adversary; someone who realizes he is facing law enforcement and/or a security presence and is clearly being patient and methodical in planning of the operation. As such, this should be factored into the overall threat assessment analysis.

Once the believed target of a threat is known to be secured in some form or fashion, the assessment of the threat, risk, etc., can begin in earnest. Decisions can be made to make contact with the threatening party and the one receiving the order. In many cases this maybe the only way to truly confirm a threat, while at the same time sending a powerful message to both parties. Depending on the nature of the threat and totality of the circumstances, it is often important to include a skilled and experienced mental health professional in the decision-making processes. This is in part due to the fact that the notification of the suspect can have an empowering effect on them, rather than discouraging them. As the end of the work day approaches, decisions can begin to be made as to the protective response deemed to be most applicable immediately and long term.

At some point, however, every protective operation will come to an end. In many cases, it is because the threat has been effectively neutralized. However, in some cases, either the threat is never fully identified and/or confirmed or simply becomes aged, as the threat is never carried out. It is these cases where making the decision to cut back or stopping the protection all together can be complicated.

> *Case in point:* On Tuesday, November 18, 1986, at around 4:00 p.m. in San Rafael, California, a man armed with a shotgun and pistol walked into a small law office, and forced the secretary to take him to where William O. Weissich was seated. As the two entered the office of Weissich, who was seated at his desk, the assassin opened fire. Weissich, who had been the district attorney for Marin County from 1953 through 1960, died at the scene. The killer, later identified as Malcolm Roland Schlette (then 77 years of age), had been sent to a long prison term for arson in 1955 (31 years prior to the attack) by Weissich. The secretary was unharmed in the attack. Schlette fled the scene in his car, which had been parked nearby prior to the killing.
> During the ensuing pursuit by law enforcement, Schlette stopped his vehicle on Highway 101 and committed suicide by swallowing cyanide. During a search of his residence, among his possessions was a list of five people Schlette believed had a role in sending him to prison. On that list was Weissich. Schlette had been previously released in 1975, and at the time prison officials advised Weissich of the threats Schlette had made towards him. At some point after his initial release, Schlette was arrested for being a felon in possession of a firearm, while trying to purchase a World War II era bazooka. At the time of the murder, Schlette was on probation for that crime.[3]

The attack on the former Marin County District Attorney William O. Weissich is perhaps the most extreme case in history in determining the presence of a threat and the amount of protection a person can reasonably be provided. Short of a 24/7 physical protective detail, the potential target should be provided with the information they need to protect themselves. Depending on the person, this can be extensive or require very little help. Therefore, it is suggested that a standard be developed.

The levels of physical protection progress until reaching the maximum level, which is, of course, a full-time security detail in armored vehicles moving from one hardened location to the next. Herein lies one of the more difficult decisions to make with such a wide spectrum of possibilities from which to choose: What to provide? Perhaps the most common is the proverbial "driver/guard." Historically, it is unknown in most cases the level of training the lone protector has had beyond just chauffeur level skills. However, even if highly skilled, providing effective protection on a sustained basis is asking a lot from a single individual. The lone operator then should rarely be used, perhaps regulated only to ensuring that a low-risk person (i.e., witness) gets from point A to point B on time and/or providing peace of mind (i.e., office staff), when little threat is known or believed to exist.

166

The ideal minimum level of physical protection should be the two-person team. This allows for the greatest flexibility and highest protection in the smallest package. One acts as a driver, the other "the eyes" on the surroundings. As the vehicle arrives and departs, one can quickly get into a protective position while driver and protectee enter or exit. While on foot, one can monitor the front and flanks while the second can control the protectee and monitor the 6 o'clock position. Beyond this, the number of protective individuals can range up to seven or more. Obviously, the more personnel, the more formidable layered security ring is in place around the protectee.

When traveling in vehicles, a two-person detail would most likely be in a single vehicle (however, not always). With three or more protectors, a second vehicle should be employed. Even if the second vehicle only has one protective member, it can still act as an advance vehicle into an area prior to arrival of the detail. It also can hold back, acting as a tail vehicle for use as a blocking element. Again, as covered in Chapter 8, this vehicle use/arrangement should be switched up to avoid patterns. Obviously, with the increased number of protective members, so, too, does the number of vehicles.

As has already been mentioned, there are many levels and types of physical protection for a protective unit to choose from. Ideally, the level of protection should be consistent with the level of threat present. Unfortunately, that is not always possible and, therefore, the decision is based on what can be provided. In many cases, the use of a physical detail is not possible. Fortunately, there are other possibilities that act as force multipliers and should be considered:

Closed circuit television (CCTV) established at a protectee's residence can be a very useful tool depending upon how it is employed. It can be positioned in such a way as to have a deterrent effect against hostile activity. CCTV also can be set up in such a way as to hide or disguise it from easy identification for use in a surveillance detection mode. With the advent of being able to check the camera offsite via Internet, protective personnel are provided with a means of keeping watch without necessarily being at the location.

Passive protective surveillance is a tool that can perhaps allow an agency to extend its protective coverage over a greater period of time or in between the period of full coverage and limited coverage. It requires a team to do a fair amount of background checking into the areas in which the principal lives and frequents. Such things as identities of neighbors within the immediate area and along the initial routes of travel into and out of the residential area should be determined. Photos and descriptions of vehicles normally in these areas need to be taken and reported.

The benefit of this tool is that a majority of the required information will be generated during the initial site survey/protective advance. Armed with the information, members of a protective unit can make periodic sweeps of the area during those times hostile activity is most likely to occur. They can even occasionally follow an individual home or to the office looking for possible hostile surveillance. (It would be a good idea to warn the individual of this prior to conducting.) The plan will be updated and modified as the operation progresses until a protective presence is no longer required. Over a period of time without any signs of a hostile presence, the operation is finally curtailed. The information used during the operation is then provided to the targeted individual as part of his/ her personal protection plan (which will be discussed in detail later in this chapter).

Utilization of local law enforcement to conduct extra patrols in the area also should be considered as a potential option (not parked in front of the residence). This could be especially useful if the law enforcement agency has the license plate reading devices (allowing near instantaneous reading of plates for detection of stolen vehicles) that are becoming increasingly common. The use of stolen vehicles for use in targeted attacks is well documented around the world.

Concealed weapons permits (CCW) and weapons at home are alternatives that can cause some sleepless nights for administrators and protective unit leaders. Should the principal be given a weapon and/or allowed to carry it in a concealed fashion? Should the principal be either issued a weapon for home protection or told to buy one if they ask (and they will ask)? Having a weapon inside the home is an issue for the target and his/her family to decide. It can be seen as the panacea for dealing with a threat, but the problem comes down to how that weapon is to be used. There are certainly historical facts connected with targets defending themselves in the home from a hostile attacker. Perhaps the most recent was the attack on Fred Capps, a prosecutor in Kentucky, by a defendant. Ultimately, Capps succeeded in stopping the attack by the killing of suspect Eddie Vaughn, but at the loss of his own life. However, he did save his family, so ultimately he could be considered successful.[4]

Beyond the potential liability issues (it is highly recommended that legal advice be sought before making this decision), the decision to provide a targeted individual with a weapon and a permit to carry it concealed is a very murky scenario. First and foremost, what type of training will be required and/or provided? What is the firearm skill level of the protectee? Shooting a number of rounds on a static line at set distances is certainly not enough. Carrying a concealed weapon and being able to effectively deploy it under stress requires a considerable amount of time and practice to perform effectively. This skill then must be maintained.

> *Case in point:* On Wednesday, October 17, 2001, at approximately 7 a.m., in Jerusalem, tourism minister and retired army General Rehavam Ze'evi was assassinated by members of the Popular Front for the Liberation of Palestine (PFLP) terrorist organization. The attack occurred inside the Jerusalem Hyatt hotel. The general was walking back toward his room after having had breakfast in the hotel restaurant. As he neared the door to his room, one of two assassins closed the distance and fired a suppressed weapon three times striking the general in the head and neck area.
>
> It was later discovered that the general had noted the presence of a suspicious man during breakfast and had mentioned it to his wife, but nothing was done beyond that. The general had also refused a protective detail, in part because of his military background. Further, he was known to carry a concealed weapon for protection. While from the information available, he apparently never had a chance to pull his weapon and fight back, he was found to have violated a major rule in self protection. When one of the assassins was later captured, it was revealed that they had discovered then the general favored this hotel and always stayed in a particular room.[5]

Regardless of the decision that is reached, under no circumstances should a protectee be armed while in the presence of a protective detail. Generally speaking, the protectee's skill with a weapon is not known, but presumably is not up to the level of the operators. Second, the person has not trained with the team and is not familiar with its methods of operation. As such, the team does not know how the protectee will react in a hostile attack, and the chances of him or her injuring a member of the detail or themselves is much greater.

Home fortification. It is truly remarkable how there is a general lack of basic security consciousness with many members of society. This becomes very apparent during security inspections of a principal's home. When a person receives a threat in the office, or a victim/witness is to be provided protection, a personal security vulnerability analysis should be offered to that individual. This should ideally occur during the initial work up of a threat assessment and/or protective operation planning. The individual being targeted should be provided with suggestions on basic fortifying methods for their home and security methods for themselves and their family members. For obvious reasons, I would not suggest providing this information to witnesses, victims, and informants if they fall into that category of "crook last week, victim/witness this week, a crook the next week … ."

The residence should be examined from the perspective of how an adversary would most likely conduct his attack. As it is exceedingly rare for a targeted attack to occur inside of a residence, the initial goal should be to strengthen the exterior to allow for the target to shelter in place, and to wait out the attack for the ultimate arrival of law enforcement. With that in mind, items should be considered, such as a quality-constructed front door, a door lock, and deadbolt mechanism on all exterior doors, including the one leading from the house to an attached garage (check, as it is not uncommon to find these doors being of the hollow core design). Locking mechanisms of some configuration on all windows and sliding glass doors is also highly recommended, especially for those windows habitually left partially open allowing for airflow.

With the vast majority of attacks worldwide occurring during the morning and evening hours[6] at the residence, generally between the front door and the street, the issue of exterior lighting cannot be over emphasized. The use of motion sensitive lighting should be positioned at a minimum near all residence entrance points as well as areas vehicles will be parked during period of nonuse. Exterior lighting should be extended to backyards, but this is not as important. In addition to the window locks, all windows should be equipped with some sort of window covering. This is especially important during the hours of darkness as anyone outside will be provided the ability to monitor activity occurring inside with very little chance of detection by those inside. Another suggestion is to have the fuse box moved into the house or garage.

Alarms systems can provide a false sense of security, but are an effective supplement to home fortification. Many security systems allow for "panic" buttons to activate audible or silent alarms. Some panic buttons can be carried on a key fob. When linked to the local police department that is already aware of a threat, they can allow for a quicker response.

Attack by snipers at the residence would seem to be a rare occurrence, but, interestingly, there have been a number of such attacks staged around the world over the decades. While installing bullet-resistant glass is not really an option, there are new materials on the market that can be applied to a window to strengthen it, at least to keep it from being smashed opened. Ironically, it has been the absence or lack of use of a single item that has

170

allowed for sniper attacks to be effectively carried out: window coverings. If drapes or blinds had been installed and used, the sniper would never have been able to see the target.

Case in point: On Monday, April 1, 1991, at approximately 11:30 p.m., in Dusseldorf, Germany, wealthy German industrialist and president of a state agency, Detlev Karsten Rohwedder, was assassinated. He was seated in his study when he was struck by three rounds fired from a high-powered rifle, one striking him in the shoulder, the second into the back, and the third through his heart. A fourth round was also fired, which struck his wife, a judge in her own right. It was later discovered that the sniper had positioned himself near a bench in a small public garden area, not 60 meters away, as evidence by four casings left at the scene along with a small piece of paper with a symbol of the Red Army Faction terrorist organization.[7]

As part of the check of the exterior, the vegetation needs to be reviewed. Is there dense foliage around windows that allow for an intruder to make entry without being visible from the sidewalk and street? Is there dense foliage around the doors and/or garage that could enable a person to lay in wait for a quick attack? If there are portions of the fence line, either the side yard or in the backyard that for one reason or another cannot be protected, such as one shared with a commercial area, recommend plants with large thorns such as a roses, or better yet, bougainvillea in moderate climates.

Mail bombs. One aspect of protection that can be easily overlooked is dealing with the prospect of explosives sent in the mail, or even left on a doorstep. While a rare method of attack, they are certainly not without precedent in the United States. The great difficulty with this style of attack is that, like a good ambush, it comes as a complete surprise. Mixed in with the millions of letters and packages being moved every day, a small but deadly explosive device can be easy to overlook.

Case in point: On Thursday, June 24, 2010, in Athens, a parcel disguised as a gift box of sweets was delivered to the Public Order Ministry building, addressed to the Public Order Minister Michalis Chrysohoidis on the seventh floor. A close friend and the head of the minister's protective detail, police officer Giorgos Vassilakis began to inspect the package prior to bringing it the final three meters into the office, when the explosive device inside detonated. The blast instantly killed Officer Vassilakis; however Chrysohoidis, who was in his office at the time, was unhurt. While there was no forewarning of the attack, Chrysohoidis was known to be a target as a result of his direct involvement in the successful take-down of the November 17 terrorist organization in 2002.[8]

While it would be all too easy to dismiss this attack out of hand due to its occurrence in a foreign country, it should be noted that Greece has not experienced such an attack in many years. More importantly, it was not that long ago that the United States was terrorized by Theodore "Ted" Kaczynski, better known as the "Unabomber" (an acronym for "university" and "airline bomber"). From his dank shed in the middle of a Montana forest, Kaczynski reached out and struck his targets with lethal efficiency. For the 17 years between 1978 and 1995, Kaczynski mailed 16 improvised explosive devices to university professors, airline officials, computer store owners, and executives that successfully killed 3 and injured another 23.

While there has been a great deal of information provided on what to look for on suspicious packages, how often is it really used? Fortunately, given the mode of delivery, these devices do not generally have any sort of antidisturbance-triggering mechanism (except for those perhaps left at a location on a ruse of being legitimately delivered). Hence, they do not generally detonate upon handling, but rather are triggered upon opening. For the protective unit, if the threat is deemed to come from antigovernment groups, right-wing religious extremist movements, or animal and environmental groups, then some time should be spent reeducating the threatened individual and family of the possibility of this type of attack

Eventually, whether by the target's own accord, or due to budgetary constraints, manpower, or even just through the passing of time without incident, protectees will be on their own. As was detailed in the William Weissich case, it is not always possible to know with any certainty if a threat has dissipated. An agency, therefore, should provide targeted individuals with enough information so as to be able to provide for their own security and, more important, be in a position to be able to recognize the indicators of a potential hostile presence.

Personal protection plans. Regardless of the reasoning, for the termination of a physical protection (if ever provided) detail, or if a threat was never able to be completely authenticated, individuals should be provided with the necessary information to protect themselves. While for those in security and law enforcement, self protection may seem to be common sense, it can be surprising how people are largely unaware (see the case in point of the Marco Biagi hit detailed in Chapter 9 for an example of this). A reference guide for the former protectee/target of what to look for, indicators of possible hostile intent, etc., can go a long way to increasing his/her knowledge and perhaps at the same time lessen a organization's liability in the future.

The aforementioned private intelligence company, STRATFOR, is a strong advocate of self-protection as a viable alternative to long-term physical security details. They have broken down their plan into four elements: that of assessment, analysis and planning, training, and, finally, practice and drilling.[9] In many cases, much of the work for a personal protection plan is completed during the initial stages of any quality protection operation. These plans also provide the opportunity for a law enforcement or security organization to be proactive in their goal of protection. What is meant by this is that in those instances where there is no known threat, but for the individuals, such as department heads or those in particular positions (i.e., gangs, narcotics, corruption units), likely to receive threats, a protective plan could be developed in advance.

The first step in a personal protection plan is the assessment of perceived and/or known threats to a targeted individual. (This also could be expanded to include all threats, such as civil and natural disasters as well as general criminal activity.) If the person has been threatened by a hostile organization, then obviously the focus should be initially there, but with the passing of time it should be expanded to include other possible, albeit unknown, threats. If prepared for department heads, then the analysis needs to be focused on all possible hostile organizations known to operate in the area and capable and/or willing to carry out such an attack.

The second step in the process is where the bulk of the work is conducted by an organization. It involves the analysis of vulnerabilities of the potential victim, of the person's cyber exposure, route analysis, surveillance detection workups, and physical site surveys. What information is currently available on the person such as photos, links to family members, details on current residence location, upcoming events, etc.? In-depth interviews with the protectee should be conducted to identify others who have ready access to the individual's schedule and/or residence. This can include extended family members, neighborhood friends, housekeepers, yard maintenance, pool cleaners, and secretarial staff. Anyone known to have access to the residence and schedule of the protectee should be assessed as a potential information source of an adversary.

For those in law enforcement, use the same techniques you would employ to search for a fugitive. While it would be comforting to know that the computerized department of motor vehicles information is secure, in reality it is not. Additionally, hostile organizations can gain access to the various "paid" public records databases, such as LexisNexis® and others. While the information available from such companies is not as easy to acquire as open source, it is obtainable and needs to be considered (again by analysis of the threat source).

As part of this stage, a route analysis is conducted on all roadways routinely traveled by the individual between office and residence, as well as frequented locations (i.e., gym, children's school, and day care, etc.). This, of course, requires individuals honestly detailing the route(s) they travel, including the admission of taking the same way to and from work. As part of this analysis, in addition to identifying those locations offering an adversary the greatest benefits and, therefore, likely ambush spots, possible routes of escape for the target will be noted. It is also recommended that, given a person's likelihood to continue with their routine of traveling the same way every day, some slight variations that are simple to travel should be provided. (While this is not ideal, the fact is that people are creatures of habit and with the passage of time, will fall back into their habits.)

A surveillance detection plan is critical and one of the most vital part of the entire personal plan. The goal is to identify those locations that a hostile surveillance presence is most apt to set up around residential, work, and frequented locations. It differs, however, from that which would be created for a protective detail in that it is a bit more simplistic. A brief explanation of the surveillance process should be provided in order for the individual to obtain an understanding of how a hostile surveillant will need to stage an ambush near the residence, office, or frequented location in terms of when the target usually arrives or leaves. The goal is to allow for the individual and/or his or her family to be able to visually sweep these locations prior to and during their initial departing from and arriving at a residence, office, etc. While this will obviously not catch the more sophisticated adversaries, it is a start in the development of their situational awareness and surveillance detection skills.

A physical site survey completes this stage of the process and, if not completed when the initial threat was received, needs to be conducted. While covered in detail above in this chapter, it is important for the targeted individual to know he/she is secure at home and in the office. As part of this, an assessment of the abilities of the local authorities in responding to the scene in the case of an emergency needs to be made.

Once all of the information has been collected and analyzed, it is put into a bespoke plan that is easy to understand and implemented. It should begin with a detailed explanation of the cycle an attack takes. (In the author's opinion, the explanation of the attack cycle should be given to any threatened party during the initial stages of a threat assessment.)

Realizing there is a process that an adversary will take, whether conducted within a few hours or a few months, can remove a considerable amount of mystery from the equation. The plan should identify the areas that hostile activity is most apt to be detected, but that it is generally not possible to determine what phase the adversary is in (this should include the statistic that most attacks occur at or near the residence location). They should be advised not take confrontational action against a possible threat, but they should attempt to obtain a license plate, a description of the car or person witnessed whenever possible and then notify police and/or office security personnel.

The next section of the plan will detail the amount of cyber exposure found to be readily available on the individual and methods or means of reducing such. This can include locking down social networking sites the individual and family use (this is especially important if children are present as they can often give out information without realizing the great benefit it provides to an adversary). The importance of not advertising travel in advance on such sites, even with family and friends (especially for children) must be reinforced. It is here that the individual receiving the plan can be informed of the issues of the various paid information services available that will have detailed information about them.

The plan moves on to detailing the weaknesses identified at the home and suggestions to strengthen them. This should include the use of cross-cut shredders for documents, coupled with a locking up of the trash barrels, which are taken to the curb the morning of pick up to lessen the likelihood of "dumpster diver" activities. Along with this, a suggestion should be made to move the mail delivery to a post office box to prevent loss and/or manipulation by a hostile party. The removal of a telephone number listed in the phone book, while increasingly rare, should be suggested.

A surveillance detection plan is provided, ideally with an overhead aerial of the residence area identifying the most likely positions a hostile party would set up on static surveillance. The individual should be advised to scan these hostile surveillance positions while still in the home if at all possible, otherwise upon leaving the home. This surveillance detection plan could be expanded to include areas along a route from home to the office that the potential victim has to travel regardless of what route is taken (generally within about 500 meters of the office or residence). It is also suggested that photos be taken of the residence from these potential surveillance points to identify what can be viewed from them.

The plan then details the routes identified as traveled by the target. It details the identified weaknesses, such as choke points, stop signs, etc., along with suggestions on how to travel these routes in the safest way possible. It also should detail secondary and tertiary routes with identification of the closest police departments along the way in case of the need to escape.

Ideally, the plan should include some of the more basic steps of self protection/awareness while driving. This includes such things as when coming to a stop behind another vehicle, making sure that the rear tires of the car in front are visible where they touch the pavement in order to provide enough maneuvering room should a rapid escape need to be made. Driving in the center lane whenever possible provides two benefits. The first gives the driver a potential avenue of escape. The second forces an adversary on foot to cross lanes of traffic in order to attack. Make sure the gas tank never drops below one third full. Keep the doors locked at all times. These are simple things that are easily done, yet not often known or implemented by the average citizen. (I have told some individuals, in an effort to get them more security conscious, that by being aware of their surroundings in a vehicle they are, as an ordinary citizen, also more likely to see that black and white vehicle behind them to remind them they are speeding.)

In some of the more urban areas of the country, public transportation is the preferred if not the only way of travel to and from an office. Unfortunately, given the nature of public transport, it is rife with issues regarding situational awareness, routes of travel, times of travel, etc. Public transportation is, in a word, the *antithesis* of everything protective units seek to avoid. If at all possible, make every attempt to dissuade a potential target from traveling by such means. A protective detail would negate the need, but in those instances where the threat cannot be confirmed or it becomes time to call off the physical protection, it behooves the person to find other means.

Public transportation involves massive amounts of people legitimately waiting in a central location for the arrival and departure at a set time. The transport makes predetermined stops at predetermined times to allow people to enter and exit. As easily as the terrorists conducted the bombings of the trains in Spain and the "tubes" in London, they could target an individual. Even if the adversary decided not to carry out a hit at such a transportation platform, they allow for relatively easy surveillance coupled with several more attack location possibilities.

Case in point: On Monday, September 25, 1995, around 7 p.m., in Boston, Massachusetts, United States Assistant Attorney General for Suffolk County Paul R. McLaughlin was assassinated. McLaughlin was on his way home, walking through a parking lot toward his car, having just exited a commuter train, when a man wearing a hooded jacket approached and opened fire. At the time of the attack, McLaughlin was prosecuting one of the leaders of a very dangerous street gang as part of Boston's first antigang violence unit. It was reported that prior to the killing, the gang had attempted unsuccessfully to kill a key witness and so turned to the prosecutor.[10]

If public transportation is to be used, then it should be switched up whenever and wherever possible. This means arriving at different times to take different trains and/or buses. This means entering and exiting at different stops, both before and after the most logical ones. Finally, this means staying alert while traveling, not working on a laptop or with the head in a newspaper, but paying attention to the immediate surroundings.

The plan should end with a reminder that it rests with the individual to implement the plan and obtain training if at all possible. If they never check the potential hostile surveillance points, if they never travel a different route to and from work, if they always walk while looking at the ground, talking on the phone, etc., rather than paying attention to their surroundings, it is likely only a matter of time before they will become victims.

Cases in point: On Monday, October 5, 1970, at approximately 8:30 a.m. in Montreal, British Trade Commissioner James Cross was kidnapped by members of Quebec's domestic terrorist organization known as the Liberation Front or FLQ. Earlier that morning two women arrived in the area of the residence of Cross and set up surveillance in order to ensure they did not miss his leaving for his habitual morning walk. The rest of the team consisting of four men armed with a revolver and three machine guns arrived in the area at approximately 8:20 a.m. in a taxi, at which point the two women left the immediate area. As Cross left this residence, the four men ambushed him and forced him into a taxi in which he was transported to a "safe house" and held for 60 days.[11]

On Saturday, October 10, 1970, at approximately 6:18 p.m. in Montreal, Minster of Labor Pierre Laporte was kidnapped by members of another cell of the FLQ terrorist organization. The attack occurred as Laporte was outside of his home playing a game of catch with his nephew. A telephone call was placed to the residence whereupon the caller was told Laporte was out front. Shortly afterwards, four well-armed terrorists arrived and kidnapped him at gunpoint. Seven days later, Laporte's strangled-to-death body was recovered in the trunk of a car at a local airport.[12]

Regardless of the level of protection to be provided, if at all, an effort must be made to help potential targets/victims to develop their situational awareness. As a part of this, it is important to examine a person's routines, habits, etc. These two cases, as with many others over the past 60 years occurred in the area of the residence. However, these highlight two areas that might easily be overlooked by a security team and/or targeted individual, that of activity on a front lawn and/or exercise. If hitting the gym is the routine, then the location obviously needs to be examined as a frequented location. If, however, the principal is an avid runner, you have a whole other set of issues. Avid runners, in my experience, generally run before or after work from either the residence or office. Runners generally go out for between 2 and 10-mile runs, depending on their conditioning. While they track their time, they also tend to run a route with which they are familiar. During months of longer nights and shorter days, the potential problems are only compounded. While you may be able to get these folks to run on a treadmill for a period of time, odds are it will not be long before they head out again.

An important aspect to giving the potential victim the knowledge and tools to provide for their own protection is to conduct periodic follow-up meetings. These meetings allow the protective team to assess that target's state of mind, and identify changes in protective needs and new information that has perhaps developed since the plan was provided. It can be surprising what the human mind can dismiss out of hand as not a threat or indication of hostile activity.

> *Case in point:* In 2003 in Sonoma County, California, a man held in the county jail on charges of domestic violence and stalking charges (with a criminal history, as well as antigovernment views) contacted his family members in a effort to locate the residence of the deputy district attorney and "stop her" from prosecuting the case. A threat/risk assessment was conducted, and the prosecutor was advised of the information and provided security tips. Over time the threat diminished, but at some point while driving home from the office, the prosecutor's vehicle was struck by an object. Upon her arrival at home, the vehicle was inspected and a bullet hole was discovered with fragments in the trunk.
>
> Amazingly, the prosecutor waited four days before advising her management or law enforcement of the incident as she did not want to bother anyone! The threat/risk assessment and investigation into the shooting ramped up immediately. Ultimately it was found to be a completely unrelated incident. The shooter was found to be a 15-year-old boy who was taking random shots at passing vehicles with a .22 caliber rifle.[13]

No matter what level of protection is ultimately provided, it is important to remember that these individuals being threatened or suspected of being targeted, and their families, will be frightened. This fear of the targets' will only be compounded if they have a family to worry about. Providing security surveys and protective plans can go a long way in giving them a certain amount of inner security as you remove some of the unknown and giving them more control of the situation.

ENDNOTES

1. Iason Athanasiadis, Assassination in Athens, published in the *Global Post*, July 20, 2010, www.globalpost.com/5572096.
2. Drug Gang Hit Man Narrates Assassination of Prosecutor in Mexico, *LA Times World*, July 13, 2010, www.latimesblogs.latimes.com/laplaza/2010/07/video-sicario-mexico-juarez.html.
3. Around the Nation: Grudge of 31 Years Ends in Murder and Suicide, AP, November 20, 1986, *The New York Times*, www.nytimes.com/1986/11/20/us/around-the-nation-grudge-of-31-years-ends-in-murder-and-suicide.html.
4. McGovern, Glenn, *Targeted Violence: A Statistical and Tactical Analysis of Assassinations, Contract Killings and Kidnappings*, CRC Press, Boca Raton, FL, 2010.
5. Israeli Minister Assassinated by staff, *The Guardian*, October 17, 2001, http://www.guardian.co.uk/world/2001/oct/17/israel2.
6. McGovern. Ibid.
7. German Far Left Dogs New Agency by Stephen Kinzer, *New York Times*, April 5, 1991, http://www.nytimes.com/1991/04/05/world/german-far-left-dogs-new-agency.html.
8. Package Bomb Kills Officer at Greek Police Ministry by Petros Giannakouris, Associated Press, *AOL News*, www.aolnews.com/world/article/package-bomb-kills-officer-at-greek-police-ministry/19530194.
9. Self-Protection: Assessing Threats and Vulnerabilities, May 31, 2006, Self-Protection: Analysis and Planning, June 1, 2006, STRATFOR, www.stratfor.com/self_protection_assessing_threats_and_vulnerabilites and www.stratfor.com/self_protection_analysis_and_planning.
10. Killer Sought in Boston Death of Gang Prosecutor by Elizabeth Mehren, *Los Angeles Times*, September 27, 1995, http://articles.latimes.com/1995-09-27/news/mn-50529_1_gang-prosecutor.
11. The October Crisis: Civil Liberties Suspended, http://archives.cbc.ca/war_conflict/terrorism/topics/101-557.
12. 1970: Canadian Minister Seized by Gunmen, *BBC On This Day*, news.bbc.co.uk/onthisday/hi/dates/stories/october/10/newsid_2531000/2531261.stm.
13. Chief Investigator Andy Mazzanti detailed this case to me, in which he had been the investigator assigned, as an example for the need of following up periodically with a targeted individual for updates (08/27/2010).

11
Conclusion

In the United States, only Secret Service agents are required to swarm their protectee and use their bodies as shields against attack. As a former Los Angeles Police Department SWAT team leader once told me, under no circumstances should any cop step in the path of a bullet for their protectee. That right/privilege should be held only for one's family, something with which I strongly concur. Protectees should be advised of this and explained that the team will do everything possible to protect the individual, but that no member of the team will intentionally take a bullet for that person.

A considerable portion of this work has dealt with preparing for the worst-case scenarios. SWAT teams train for hostage rescues; military and, increasingly, police units train to operate in chemical and biological environments even though the chances of such attacks are remote. The goal is, should the worst-case scenario become a reality, those asked to respond or operate can do so effectively and with the maximum amount of safety possible. There should be no difference in this philosophy for protective teams and, therefore, they need to train for the worst, if they are to be effective.

Most in this business, like regular cop work, will never experience a hostile attack. However, should you be one of those unfortunate few to find themselves in an ambush situation, you will be in for the fight of your life. If an adversary has deemed the target important enough to attack your protective operation, then that adversary knows that his first priority is to overcome your resistance. If you have not trained for these possibilities, then the worst-case scenario is now your grim reality. In the immortal words of Sir Winston Churchill, "Never, never, never give up."

So there you go. I hope that this work, coupled with the referenced suggested reading and training, will enable the reader and the team with the necessary groundwork to successfully provide a quality protective function. From here, the team must develop its own tactics and train for it. Remember, in this deadly game, there is no second place. Either train and be prepared to bring the fight, or walk away. As retired U.S. Army Lt. Colonel Dave Grossman stated over the course of his "Bullet-Proof Your Mind" presentation, "Denial is the enemy. The opposite of denial is acceptance and if you accept it, you prepare. Identify the worst thing that can happen and prepare for it. Nothing, but the steely performance of dedicated professionals."

Be safe and watch your six.

Glenn P. McGovern

APPENDIX A: LAW ENFORCEMENT PROTECTIVE OPERATIONS

Suggested Training and Reading

TRAINING

Explosives

"Post-Blast Investigations" is a 32-hour course put on by both the U.S. Bureau of Alcohol, Tobacco, Firearms, and Explosives (ATF) and the Federal Bureau of Investigation (FBI). It provides a good introduction into explosives, including commercial, military, and improvised, along with the various methods of triggering devices.

"Incident Response to Terrorist Bombings" is a 32-hour course developed by the U.S. Department of Homeland Security. This course provides a much more detailed examination into the use and blast effects of commercial, military, and improvised explosives. It culminates with the students assisting in the building of a 500-lb ammonium nitrate and fuel oil (ANFO) car bomb that is subsequently detonated.

"Prevention and Response to Suicide Bombing Incidents" is a 40-hour course prepared by the Department of Homeland Security that is focused entirely on the suicide bomber. A variety of improvised explosives are discussed and detonated to determine the various effects. The course culminates with a full-scale scenario and response to a simulated suicide bomber attack operation.

Snipers

One- or two-day sniper overview schools are periodically available and provide a basic understanding of the skills set. Lacking that, a one-day "basics" course on sniper and countersniper methods and tactics could easily be developed by any competently trained sniper. Every person on a protective team would benefit immensely from learning some of the intricacies a sniper deals with using a bolt-action weapon, a rifle scope, different shooting positions, hide development, etc. Ideally, a former military or SWAT sniper on a protective team could provide such training, but lacking that, reach out to a local SWAT sniper.

Driving Schools

There are a variety of quality driving schools available. Every team member should attend at least one. The Alameda County Sheriff's Office in California provides a quality one-, three-, and five-day course dealing with "Dignitary Protection Driver Training." These courses provide the student with the opportunity to learn and practice evasive driving maneuvers that could mean all the difference if a protective motorcade is ever attacked. It is only at such courses, in the proper facilities, that drivers will be able to learn forward and reverse 180° turns, and "J" turns, among a whole host of other potentially lifesaving techniques.

Surveillance Detection

"Surveillance Detection for Municipal Officials" is a 24-hour course that is put on by the Department of Homeland Security. While this course is primarily geared toward static surveillance detection, it allows teams to develop the necessary basic understanding of the surveillance detection methodology and the importance of data collection and analysis.

Threat/Risk Assessment

"Enhanced Threat and Risk Assessment" is a 16-hour course that, while focused on threats and risks faced by facilities, will assist those conducting protective advances. This practical course requires attendees to spend time out in the field at a potential target learning firsthand how to identify potential vulnerabilities that an adversary could take advantage of.

Further, the students then identify the necessary steps to correct problems and strengthen the location against attack.

READING

Protective Intelligence and Threat Assessment Investigations: A Guide for State and Local Law Enforcement, U.S. Department of Justice, July 1998.

The Al Qaida Manual is available from numerous sources via the Internet and should be required reading by all team members. It provides a wealth of tactical information, but more importantly, it provides the reader with an understanding of what their potential adversary may be training and implementing in preparation of the attack.

Mini Manual of the Urban Guerrilla by Carlos Marighella, is available online from multiple sources. It is one of the first manuals ever written from the perspective of the terrorist on conducting terrorist and insurgent operations in the urban terrain. It realizes the issues involved in dealing with a law enforcement response, maintaining cover and camouflage of the team and individual operator among many other topics.

Countering Suicide Terrorism: An International Conference, by the International Policy Institute for Counter-Terrorism at the Interdisciplinary Center, Herzliya, February 20 23, 2000,

Introduction to Executive Protection, by Dale L. June, CRC Press, Boca Raton, FL, 1999.

Surveillance Detection: The Art of Prevention, by Laura Clark and William E. Algaier, Author House, Bloomington, 2005.

On Killing: The Psychological Cost of Learning to Kill in War and Society, by Lt. Col. Dave Grossman, Back Bay Books, Boston, 1995.

Killing Zone: A Professional's Guide to Preparing or Preventing Ambushes, by Gary Stubblefield and Mark Monday, Paladin Press, Boulder, CO, 1994.

Just 2 Seconds: Using Time and Space to Defeat Assassins, by Gavin De Becker, Tom Taylor, and Jeff Marquart, Crown Publishers, New York, 2008.

Law Enforcement Counter Intelligence, by Lawrence B. Sulc, Varro Press, Kansas City, MO, 1996.

Surveillance Countermeasures: A Serious Guide to Detecting, Evading and Eluding Threats to Personal Privacy, by ACM IV Security Services, Paladin Press, Boulder, CO, 1994.

How to Look for Trouble: A Stratfor Guide to Protective Intelligence, by Stratfor Global Intelligence, Austin, TX, 2010.

The Tactical Trainer: A Few Thoughts on Training and Training Management from a Former Special Operations Soldier, by MSG Paul R. Howe, US Army Retired, Author-House, Bloomington, IN, 2009.

Combat Use of the Double-Edged Fighting Knife, by Col. Rex Applegate, Paladin Press, Boulder, CO, 1993.

DOCUMENTARIES AND FILMS

The Baader Meinhof Complex, MPI Home Video, March 30, 2010, provides some decent recreations of the vehicle ambushes perpetrated by members of the Baader Meinhof Gang, better known as the Red Army Faction or RAF. In many of these attacks, a protective detail was present consisting of cops, who were killed.

Secrets of the Dead: The Umbrella Assassin, by PBS, November 14, 2006. Details the assassination of Georgi Markov in London by members of the Bulgarian Intelligence Service.

Four Days in September, by Miramax Films 1997. Details the kidnapping of the U.S. ambassador to Brazil. Provides a good recreation of the ambush.

Ronin by MGM Studios, February 23, 1999. The fictional account of a mercenary force targeting a victim with a protective detail. Keeping in mind the "Hollywood" aspects, the film does a fantastic job in recreating a potential legitimate preparation and take-down of a target. From the initial planning on the ambush location, required equipment, order of events at the attack site, and so on (using techniques used in actual attacks from around the world).

APPENDIX B

In the following pages are samples of forms that can be used by protective teams for a whole host of different needs during a threat situation. The goal is for teams not having to reinvent the wheel when dealing with these situations. Feel free to copy and modify them, and make your own. These are provided only as suggestions.

Personal Security Tips—A handout that has been modified from a variety of other forms and handouts. Its purpose is to be given to a person upon the initial receipt of a threat whether determined to be legitimate or not.

Personal Medical Information—This is to be filled out by all protectees and team members prior to any protective operation. The sheets should be sealed in an envelope, signed on the seal, and provided to the team leader who holds them until the operation is completed. At that time they should be returned to the individual.

Risk Model Worksheet—A sample form that can be used in assessing the threat/risk faced by an individual.

OPSEC Spreadsheet—This sheet is designed to allow for a protective team to monitor what teams, safe houses, equipment, vehicles, etc., were used during operations in an effort to preserve operational security.

PERSONAL SECURITY TIPS

At the Residence

- Install solid wood, fiberglass, or steel doors and front entrance ways.
- Install and/or rekey all deadbolt locks on all exterior doors including between main home and garage (use only quality brands, such as Schlage).
- If new residence, perform change prior to moving in.
- A door chain is not secure and can easily be forced open; consider installation of floor-mounted door bar.

- Install locks on all windows and consider the placement of dowel rods into the window tracks to prevent easy opening.
- Install a wide-angle viewer in all exterior doors.
- Remove or thin vegetation around doors and windows (preventing someone hiding prior to attack, and allowing someone braking in to be seen by neighbors and friends.
- Install motion sensor lights on exterior of home to discourage prowling and loitering.
- On all entrances and walkways, install lights bright enough to eliminate shadows.
- Install timer switches on lights in living rooms, guest rooms, etc., to feign that the home is occupied.
- Use "no solicitors" signs at front doorways to discourage strangers from coming to the door.
- If you are going to be away from the home, have the mail stopped, or have a neighbor or friend pick it up along with the newspaper.

Key Control

- Provide a duplicate house key to relative, trusted friend, or neighbor in case of lock out.
- NEVER hide house keys in mailboxes, planters, doormats, or other locations where they can be easily discovered.
- Do not have personal identification attached to keys.
- Be able to separate vehicle key from house keys (provide valets, mechanics, etc., only with the car key)
- If keys are lost, have all locks rekeyed.

If a Stranger Is at Your Door

- Never indicate you are home alone.
- When home, try not to open the door to a stranger.
- Use wide-angle door viewers to see who is there.
- Ask to see identification of individuals at your door whom you are not familiar with (including police officers, repairmen, etc).
- Do not open the door to a stranger requesting help or the use of your telephone. Offer to make the telephone call yourself while the stranger waits outside.
- Never allow a stranger into a security entrance.
- Children should not answer the door.

- When children are home alone, all exterior window coverings should be drawn.
- Do not put names on mailboxes, but when required, only the last name.
- Remove home telephone number from telephone directory.
- Always lock the front door, even when home, but especially when you leave.
- Keep window blinds, shutters, and curtains closed when away and especially at night.

Telephone Calls

- Do not provide telephone number to "wrong telephone number" callers.
- Check references of any person seeking information about you for a survey, credit check, subscription drive, etc.
- If you receive a threatening, harassing, or obscene telephone call, make note of the time of the call and what was said. Then notify the police department, request a police report, then contact your telephone company.

Intruders

- If you are home and you suspect someone is trying to break in, call law enforcement immediately by dialing 911.
- If confronted by an intruder, stay as calm as possible.
- Choose a strategy such as negotiating, fleeing, screaming, fighting, or complying, whichever seems the safest and most effective relative to the situation.

Returning Home

- As you arrive home, scan the frontage of your property. During hours of darkness, slow your vehicle in order to allow the headlights to scan as much as possible. Keep the doors locked and lights on until satisfied.
- If family are home, have them looking for your arrival and alert to what is going on. If need be, have a neighbor or friend meet you.
- When approaching the walkway/entranceway to your home, have your key in your hand and positioned to insert into the lock.

- If you note a broken window, an exterior door unlocked or open, or anything that strikes you as unusual, do not enter. Immediately leave and call 911. Let police officers check the home prior to your entering.

Walking/Jogging/Running

- Avoid doing these activities alone, especially during hours of decreased light (dawn and dusk).
- If an activity must occur during hours of reduced light, select routes that are well lit, avoiding areas of abandoned buildings, construction sites, alleyways.
- Plan out your route allowing for you to stay in areas where other people are present.
- Let a family member or trusted friend/neighbor know your route.
- Stay alert to your surroundings; observe people and activities. Wear only one earphone to your MP-3 player and do not set the music volume to loud.
- Walk, jog, or run toward traffic to allow you the ability to see approaching vehicles.
- Consider carrying a flashlight (many now come equipped with a cap designed to be used in striking) and/or pepper spray.
- Carry a personal alarm to attract attention and summon help if needed.
- If you notice a car following you, use your personal alarm, or start yelling loudly and cross the street, heading in the opposite direction if possible.

Driving

- Keep your vehicle in good working order.
- Never allow the gas tank to drop below a quarter full.
- Keep the doors locked at all times.
- Plan your route in advance when unfamiliar with the area.
- Keep valuables out of sight.
- Drive in the center lanes of traffic when possible.
- Keep windows up whenever possible, especially when driving in areas of reduced speeds.
- Never pick up hitchhikers.

- If you see another motorist in trouble on the side of the road, do not stop, but rather call for assistance.
- If a vehicle tries to force you off the road, do not stop; continue driving to the nearest open business, police station, or fire station. If possible note the vehicle license plate number and vehicle description as well as that of the driver and passengers.

Parking

- Select well-lit parking areas whenever possible.
- Look around prior to unlocking the doors and exiting the vehicle.
- Be especially cautious and alert in underground, stacked, or enclosed parking areas.
- Whenever possible, make use of valet parking.

Automated Teller Machine (ATM)

- Whenever possible, select an ATM in a shopping mall, market, or on a busy street.
- Have your card and any paperwork ready when you get up to the machine.
- Be alert to people loitering around the ATM and in nearby parked vehicles.
- If you are uncomfortable, leave and go to another location to safely conduct your business.
- Do not sit in the car at the ATM to conduct your personal accounting.
- Protect your Personal Identification Number (PIN) from being seen by others.

Public Transportation

- Use only well lit, frequently used bus stops, train/subway stations and taxi stands whenever possible.
- Do not wait alone at a bus stop, train/subway station, or taxicab stand.
- Be alert to who gets on and off a bus, train, or subway with you.
- If you believe you are being followed, inform other passengers, the driver, or other uniformed individuals and request assistance.

At Work

- When possible, walk with other people between the office and your parked vehicle.
- If a suspicious person follows you into the elevator, immediately step out.
- When inside an elevator, stand by the control panel to allow quick access to the alarm button in an emergency.
- If you must work late hours, alert a family member, friend, or security officer. If possible have the security officer check on your status.
- If leaving the office late in the evening, request a security officer (if available) to escort you to your car or public transportation.
- Report all suspicious persons and activity to security personnel, even if not until the following day.

If a Hostile Individual Approaches You

Every situation is different and requires a different response that can only be determined as it happens. Keep assessing the situation and think. Be confident, even if in appearances only, and never ever give up. Try stalling for time, negotiating, and being verbally assertive. Try distracting the adversary and fleeing. If someone is attempting to force you into a vehicle, fight and resist with every ounce of energy you have. Let all of your anger come to the surface and do everything possible to prevent being taken. Scream at the top of your lungs and attack the vulnerable parts of the attacker's body.

ADVERSARY INTELLIGENCE SHEET

		Proven	Estimated
Who are the adversaries?			
What is their intent?			
What is their area of operations?			
What is their intelligence collection capability?	Signal		
	In person		
	Technical		
	Cyber		
	Other		
What is their access to weapons?	Explosives		
	Automatic weapons		
What is their preferred method of attack?	Drive-by		
	Close attack		
What is their preferred operational strength?	Lone attacker		
	Two or three attackers		
	Three or more attackers		
Known allies?			
What are the allies' area of operations?			
What is the allies' intelligence collection capability?	Signal		
	In person		
	Technical		
	Cyber		
	Other		
What is the allies' access to weapons?	Explosives		
	Automatic weapons		

MEDICAL FORM

DATE:
NAME:
DATE OF BIRTH:
BLOOD TYPE:
MEDICATION ALLERGIES:
CURRENT MEDICATIONS:
MEDICAL CONDITIONS:
EMERGENCY CONTACT:

RISK MODEL WORKSHEET

| Threat | Threat Factors | | | | Threat Level (1–8) | Method of Attack: A, firearms; B, sniper; C, explosives |
	Existence (1)	Violent History (1)	Intentions (2)	Targeting (4)		
1						
2						
3						
4						
5						
6						
7						
8						
9						
10						

OPSEC SPREADSHEET

Date	Name	Organization	Vehicles Used	Weapons	Team Members	Locations	Routes

INDEX

For Product Safety Concerns and Information please contact our
EU representative GPSR@taylorandfrancis.com Taylor & Francis
Verlag GmbH, Kaufingerstraße 24, 80331 München, Germany